Everything
Is
Something
Else

New and Selected Poems
1989-2019

poems by

Franco D'Alessandro

Finishing Line Press
Georgetown, Kentucky

Franco D'Alessandro

BrV/21

Spiral Tree © Susan Benarcik

Everything
Is
Something
Else

New and Selected Poems
1989-2019

For Wo Chan and my friends at Lambda Literary,

Enjoy these poems and the pieces of my queer soul on these pages!

Avanti!
Ar aghaidh!

Trebor

Publisher: Leah Huete de Maines

Editor: Christen Kincaid

Cover Art: Susan Benarcik: "Spiral Tree" (cover)

Interior Art: Susan Benarcik

Author Photo: Jane Santos

Cover Design: Franco D'Alessandro

Page 80: Tennessee Williams and Anna Magnani, Creative Commons
License 2.0

Order online: www.finishinglinepress.com
           also available on amazon.com

Author inquiries and mail orders:
Finishing Line Press
P. O. Box 1626
Georgetown, Kentucky 40324
U. S. A.

Table of Contents

PART III:
FIRE TEARS / LACRIME FIAMMANTE / DEORA DÓITEÁIN

"Love is a battle, love is a war; love is a growing up...
The poet is produced by the people because the people need him."

—James Baldwin

In Loving Memory
of
my beloved Irish Mother...
do m'anam Éireannach
&
my dearest Italian Father...
per il mio cuore Italiano

For Michael—MAC,
who loves and understands,

and,

my Nieces, Nephews, Godchildren,
and God-sent student-children,
who teach and inspire me so much.

AUTHOR'S INTRODUCTION

I wrote my first poems in a marble notebook in Mary Cronin's classroom when I was 16; I was scared, lonely, queer, and—somehow—bold. I never stopped writing, and she and I forged a lifelong friendship. At the time, those poems were an outcry—to be heard, to be helped, to be seen. Today, perhaps, my work still cries out, but now it does so in order to share, to understand, to connect. In the last year of his life, Tennessee Williams said: *"What should matter most to you, is the rare and gorgeous experience of reaching out through your work and your actions and connecting to others. A message in the bottle thrown toward another frightened, loveless queer; a confused mother; a recently dejected man who can't see his way home. We get people home; we let them know that we're here for them. This is what art can do. Art should be the arm and the shoulder and the kind eyes—all of which let others know you deserve to live and to be loved. That is what matters, baby. Bringing people home."* Williams considered himself, first and foremost, a poet; his impeccably crafted phrases, intensely imagistic language, and deeply soulful themes—of longing and exile and truth—resonate with people today as much as they ever did. Through this collection, I, too, hope to be that arm, or shoulder, or kind eye for my readers; more precisely, I hope to be a sort of life-raft for the soul for those in need of a bit of salvation—of being brought home.

Conceptually, this book is divided into three different parts of my identity: the Italian, the Irish, and the Queer. I have always been fascinated by people's ethnic identities because my own is so important to me. Identifying as Italian and Irish and connecting to those cultures through my American upbringing means the world to me. But being ethnic and staying ethnic are two different things; I spent a lifetime immersed in the culture, music, language, arts, and literature of Italy and Ireland—I have always felt the obligation to earn and keep my hyphens. My Gay identity, too, matters. I was out before it was in; I was Queer before it was cool; I was perverse before it paid to be so; and I weathered a lot of ugliness since coming into myself at 17 and out to the world at 22, but nowhere on earth is it better to be LGBTQ than here in the USA. Stonewall happened here for a reason, and I am very much a child of that revolution. Those were difficult, complex, exciting times. If you came out and came up in the 1980s (during the AIDS pandemic), as I did, you lived in a shadow-dance of desire and death.

Being 50-something is a great advantage. Many times in my life, people have told me that I am too outspoken or have commented on my boldness—but what point is there in being a little outspoken? What good is a thought, if it is not a bold one? After all, a writer's job is to investigate the scorching landscape of the human soul. These varied poems, written over 30 years, aspire to achieve what many poets strive for: connection, understanding. Poetry attempts to map the landscape of the human soul—that protean terrain, at times hostile, at times hospitable—where wild hearts run free. Poetry is an act of courage. It helps us make sense of our own lives; to give meaning to unutterable events, undefinable experiences, and inexpressible emotions that are always yearning for a voice. In its brevity, immensity, lucidity, boldness, sharpness, and electricity, poetry is an exhortation to us all: *your life is a house on fire, find the courage to run in and rescue love!*

I have been writing poems longer than I have been writing plays, and 50 is an interesting age to reach as an artist; you have so much more to say but you feel that you have increasingly less time to say it. Rather prophetically, a character in a play I wrote 20 years ago said: "the only thing we gain in life is more loss." The keen—if not painful—awareness of the clock's monosyllable (where each tick announces more loss) becomes more intense and ominous at my age; you calculate everything according to the urgent and hopeful formula of, "*If I live to 100...then...*" From suicide to AIDS to Alzheimer's to cancer, I know that my own life has been defined and shaped by a series of significant and tragic losses; undoubtedly creating a significant theme in this collection of losing what we love / loving what we've lost. At the same time, many of these poems deal with identity, my struggles, and triumphs in forging my own persona in terms of sexuality and ethnicity; they all, however, seek connection and understanding. The older I get, the more I come to know in my soul that understanding is really the greatest form of love. I have had that with a few people in my life so far and in the most unlikely and enduring friendships: the cousins who are sisters; the former teacher who is a mother; the fellow artist who is a wife; the childhood friends who are family; the students who become longed-for children.

So, I am now more certain than ever that genuine understanding on the soul level is exactly what we all seek, whether we know it or not, and whether we are ready for it or not. This connection and understanding of two souls is what the Irish call *anam chara*—your soul's friend. Poetry has always been a soul friend to me, and in order for our soul friends to endure, they must speak the inaudible language of truth that is understanding. I knew so much when I was 25, and now, as I move through middle-age, while the time of my youth—when I was so certain about so many things— becomes ever more distant, I am becoming less certain of so many other things. In this world, where memories are really moments colored in with imagination and certainty diminishes as we grow older, one is reminded of—maybe even takes comfort in—William Faulkner's axiom: "The past isn't dead. It's not even past." Indeed, it seems to me—and, perhaps, to you too—that everything is something else

—**Franco D'Alessandro**
May 2020
Bronxville, New York

"Boundaries of Logic" © Susan Benarcik

FOREWORD BY PAMELA J. RADER, PH.D.

It is no accident that Franco has divided this book into three sections—a trinity of influences or a triptych of narratives that examine the influences of his maternal Irish lineage, his Italian paternity, and his identity as a Gay-Irish-Italian-American and teacher. This collection of poems is written in the vein of American confessional poetry and explores the landscapes of memory.

Readers will find poems from *Supplications* (2009) and unpublished poems. Franco revisits childhood memories and celebrates his unwavering love for his mother in several new pieces. For any reader who has tried to run away as a child, or whose attempts to run away have been thwarted, one will recognize the compassionate mother "Gliding in her silver Skylark" as the one we all want to find and bring us home. In this collection, the writer battles with the loss of a beloved parent. And the one who is slipping away, "On the way to the hospital it occurs to me:/you are not always going to be here,/Or there, where I've counted on you being for so many years." These experiences of ageing include pondering how we all lose parents and will continue to lose them again and again. For grown children who love their parents, we know we will lose them again when we go because our memory goes with us.

Memory and the tricks of time toy with us at different stages of life. There is the writer who is compelled to document family history. And there is the human being who watches and worries, in "Listening to Dylan" "When [the father is] alone, he keeps asking himself questions,/*How many times must a man?.../*but he just can't find the answers...'" The collection reveals humanity's shared nostalgia as we listen to the music we loved when we were younger and when those we loved were still with us. And it reminds us of humanity's propensity for questions asked but not always answered.

In conclusion, poetry often takes up the issue of names as we see in "That Endless Name," where the writer reflects on what it takes to find oneself, "And I've grown into the narrator,/who is merely, only, just me." Ultimately, the "me" is always in the process of becoming and being defined by the people we love and who love us in return. Franco's collection of reflections shares one man's life experiences mapped by loving.

Part I

Anam Fhuil
Soul Blood
Sangue dell'anima

"Yes: I am a dreamer. For a dreamer is one who can only find his way by moonlight, and his punishment is that he sees the dawn before the rest of the world."

—Oscar Wilde, "The Critic as Artist"

*I see this old bad order die
In a great swift blaze of fire
A structure, clear and mighty high
Born in its funeral pyre*

"They took away our land, our language, and our religion; but they could never harness our tongues."

—Brendan Behan

"Meditations" Copyright Susan Benarcik © 2020

MIND YERSELF

for my Granma, Mary McCreely Dunn Grace
le buíochas do Ciarán Carson

Suddenly, when it came time to leave,
She would always grab you by the shoulders, blue eyes brimming
      with watery fire,
And sweetly offer her exhortation; *"Mind Yerself, now..."*
She'd say, as if you were the only one
      in the world
      that mattered (and you were);
      As if it were you against the world; as if when you were
      leaving her house you were going out into a world
      that had it in for you.

She had grown up
      dragged between Belfast, Carlingford, and Liverpool;
      home was on Ardmoulin Street off
      the Falls Road; where so much fell apart,
      Stumbled and tumbled away,
      Tripped by Brits...
      She *Sean-nós*-ed between the daily, deadly raindrops that ran
      across
      the streets and plopped from the gathering gray sky.
It was a happy homeplace in a horrible home time
      and they hated to hate it as much as they did,
      During that terribly beautiful troubling time,
      50 years before *Na Trioblóidí...*
Her people were *Gaeilgeoirí*—
      a lost, voiceless people losing their language—
Home Rule, Rising, Partition she lived through...
Summer 1920, Swanzy in Lisburn...Bloody two years
When Bloody Sundays became mundane
The UVF revived to kill the survived
USC—those Ulster not-so Specials; the Orange B-men who would not be
      men;
      made the Black and Tans pale—
Then the RUC got Uncle Danny good;

his guts got spilled in 1916—*Somme*-where in France
They came for the rest, shot him on his doorstep.

Even as St Peter's Cathedral loomed in the background
—some comfort somewhere between Antrim and Armagh;
nothing settled, nothing certain...so much nothing
In the bruised beauty of Belfast,

Refuge was the family farm of clan McCann in Carlingford.
          Just beyond
                    Over the new border that no one recognized,
                    An oasis between the lough and Slieve Foye.
                    In the shadow of that Sleeping Giant—they prayed
                    would one day awake, and raise its hand
                    and take revenge for their mutilated land.

Across the pond, in Liverpool, in the land of the enemy awash in
          Éire's exiles,
an unkind ghetto of another kind;
where she and they were treated somehow inexplicably better;
or at least not assailed and assaulted—daily—
No longer dodging
The rain-drops-of bullets, the city on the Mersey
                    (that showed a bit more mercy)
Would never be home, just a lodging, a refuge...
There she found comfort in The Three Graces
who are seated on the Pier Head,
Protecting the pieces of her family who came and went;
Too many to name maimed and dead.

When your language and land and songs and dances
Have been stolen and broken,
All smashed by lost chances.
All dreams set beside the whiskey on the shelf.
You earn everything, And you learn—you must learn—
to *mind yourself.*

She rode a river of blood to the Bowery in 1927,
Where 4 people lived in a 2-room tenement.
Where, at 16, she once beat a man
with her father's shillelagh for touching her
Convent-bound, baby sister.
She had minded herself, since the day she was born
What greater love is there than self-care?
And now, with her 13 grandchildren
—this woman, who made herself, her life, all she had
        From the love she made,
        From Irish grit,
        From Celtic fire,
        From her soul's blood...*fuil an anam*...

All this, suddenly,
all of this was in her voice
        at 60 and 70 and 80...
It always came a second time.
        It had to—
After a sigh that weighed as much
as all those cries and years:
        "...*Mind yerself!*"
And then, the embrace, one that held all
Those fugitives and relatives,
The hunted and haunted,
The beaten, chased, and disgraced
across three countries...To here,
Now...
        ...*Mind yerself*...is Irish
        for
I love you.

TERRIBLE BEAUTIES

for W. B. Yeats and
for all of us who came out when the stakes were
so high and the cost so dear

My love is a rock
Thrown at the marching moral monsters;
I am (as Baldwin said)
    Only free in battle...

I am the shadow of the rock—a bloodied shadow of love,
Who refuses the passionless prison
of a quiet existence.
   Undetected...
Until it's thrown.
    And then felt.

A shadow of love's bloody rock
Like my Irish ancestors, under centuries
Of brutal subjugation.

   No; I, too, am a rock
   —a nameless, shameless rock—
   Born from that shadow;
   Made of love and hardness,
   and forbidden freedom,
Heavenly hurled
To give birth to more
Terrible beauty.

IRISH SLAP

for my brothers

My brother told me, recently,

> how she stood listening to him
> gnawing on the bones and sinew
> and savory fat of his
> brother's failures—the Bohemian bon vivant
> who lived on borrowed money in a borrowed time,
> writing "poems" or "plays"—hanging out with
> queers and gays—he grew enraged at his own words
> And she, increasingly, bruised by them...

> Then, without a word or wince
> of warning
> She leapt across the kitchen
> —her domain over which she reigned
> for decades—
> and slapped his mouth full-stop,

> As if to swat at a malevolent flying insect
> whose sole buzzing purpose is to
> bring pain...

> As if to smack back a recently trapped
> wild animal who attempts to flee its cage
> with a threatening growl...

> As if what he said were so unforgivable
> the words had to be forced back
> inside his mouth—forever blocked, stopped, and banished
> from poisoning her ears and the loving, harmonious home
> she had built.

> Startlingly, slowly...*SLAAAP-P-P!*
> Its humbling heat hung in the air
> —the way a deliberate regret can—

A salty-sweet drop of blood
left his lips suddenly sated
Her eyes filled with blue fire;
And he grew more bold and dire.

They stood silent for a while
—Mother and son—
he, racked with guilt of fraternal betrayal;
she, sick with maternal malefaction.

A truce soon struck, he felt the fire
of that fierce Loyalty,
     that came from somewhere deep in
     Her storied DNA
     (dílseachta mháthar fíochmhar)
That limitless, relentless fire love
—born out of her primordial fear of family fissures—
was extended to him, too.

And the slap, which wasn't a slap but something else,
     for him—now that she's gone—
somehow, means so much more.

And, years after
we to soon buried her,
The feared for rift drew us closer together,
...and...
We cried in each other's arms when he told me.

WE DIDN'T YET UNDERSTAND

You didn't understand
How your pocketbook made it into the freezer,
Or how the fresh vegetables:
six carrots, a bunch of celery and four zucchini
were found at the bottom of the trash can;
the refrigerator was neatly stacked with the rotting produce
you pulled from the garbage—
colorful remnants of redolent rubbish.

"What the *hell*?!"
You did not respond to my first freaked reaction,
But remained a sea of sad calm.
As I quickly recovered and hijacked my surprise—
You stared so sweetly; as if asking a thousand questions
Whose only possible answers were hushed, eerie echoes;
As inaudible as they were ever fading...
Oh, you tried to catch at meaning with both your hands,
But logic was fragile, an evanescent spark in your Wedgwood blue eyes.
Your look, that look, was a reaching back
to hear; to understand what
Could not be comprehended; what
Could not even be expressed;
A look so helpless and terrified—
Child's eyes, you are 12 again,
Wide-eyed, watching your father die;
These tears—like bloody raindrops from an angry sky god—
Are not yours, now
They belong to the 220lb man who has
thrown his head against the wall
All his weight sliding down, thudding
against the hardwood floors.
A profusion of confusion—that salty
Unstoppable rising tide:
"How can this be happening?" as hands tear into brain
A torrent of torment that cannot be stemmed or ebbed.
Trying to find the understanding,
the scream is swallowed a hundred times

Folding into itself, knowing the only solution is
the resolution:
>   to tenderly hold the pieces and fragments of
>   you
>   Together—
>   To gather you, all of you
>   Up, and hold you again...

But you left so soon,
Your mind ran away and your soul soon followed; but
I am still haunted by your starry staring,
Still haunted by
The courage you had as you jousted with infinity
And stuck to your exit plan.
Your tender vacant visage...
not knowing what just happened, but painfully aware
of what was happening;
...But we didn't know...then;
Or perhaps we both knew but we just didn't
Yet,
>   Understand.

SHE'S LEAVING

for Mommy, Mary Julia Grace D'Alessandro

She's leaving me
                Again
                          Still
                                  More
And more
...She's leaving

I'll think about the way the snow held her perfume, *Shalimar*...
Guiding me home on frosty days
That left me lost in infinite whiteness,
In the ice cube of adolescent loneliness,
Wandering through the hollow distance,
Anticipating—
To be cherished in warm arms
 wrapping me in a hot chocolate embrace.

Lilies and tulips; those fleeting flowers
whose beginnings brightened the kitchen...
Darting out of the house to greet the coming green—
I'd run from her
Only to tumble back
with earth-stained knees
Spring hoping eternal,
Throwing baseballs and hiding
Easter eggs, which held the magic of surprises
And devotion.

I'll remember her soft, soft, smooth ceramic skin,
Which has known the salty water of joy
And sorrow,
And summer sea breezes
Vibrantly stained by time, and sun, and forward motion
hawking from the shade as
I floated away
testing the tides...

Barbecue smoke-signals calling me home.

I will always see her
Standing in the stadium,
the Roman matron, Cornelia.
Her son, the football gladiator...
Long rides along the Hudson into kaleidoscopic foliage,
leaves, a mosaic of memory—
Trying to remember;
To re-capture—
to taste her again—
to savor her pumpkin pie smile.

For now, I hold her love-stained hands
That assembled thirty thousand meals;
Her fingers smell of garlic and basil.
We pass time that has all since
passed us by
and by
This is—*Good-bye*?

While I discover the unendurable—
and uncover the irretrievable,
I try to recover those lost parts of her, but
She is still leaving me
Again
       More
            And more
In pieces...
         And I'm wondering
where the peace is?
Now, I see her as an ancient Celtic statue
Perched—skyward—on a cliff above Galway Bay;
Worn by the sea-salted air and wicked winds,
her moss mottled mind; bits of her chipped away...

My eyes cannot leave her,
That kind haunted face,
For fear I might forget her;
Knowing memory has lost this race.
And the steely sadness catches me

Again
           More
                        Still
I see her leaving in everything;
The cold, steely sadness
Escorting the woman out of the world,
Who brought me
in.

THE SANDBOX

for Edward Albee

If you must,
Go play in the sandbox
I will wait,
and understand
for a while...
but I know I will grow angry,
soon;
The sandbox
is not a place to be alone,
the vastness of the mini-desert
can be devastatingly solitary—
inside or
outside of it;
Even staring at the arid sea
of nothingness
can swallow you up,
as much as standing in it
will readily reduce you to a
memory.

       The probability of the next moment,
       More shattering
       than the possibility of this one.

But you keep staring;
As if you cannot
Help yourself...

If you must,
Bury yourself in the sand
with your little blue shovel
and broken plastic pail;
"nothing works anymore"
I hear you say to no one.

I will wander
for a while....
Seduced by the sounds of summer
Floating freely like a balloon
let loose
at the country fair
but then, I will then get sad,
suddenly,
and wonder why I didn't
kick my shoes off
and let the sand
get between my toes...
and wait with you
for the music of the Mr. Softee truck
and share the happiness of ice cream
At sunset
in July
on our street
just us two
one
last
time.

If you must.
Go play in your sandbox
And as you sink deep
into the dusty, fawn
endless, sandy sea
I will try not to miss you
...and the *you* with me.

FIRST SWIMS

for my cousins, Suzanne and Mary

Clinging, wading, wondering...
Arms tourneqetting around
her slick freckled neck.
Nose buried in cheek, nestled amidst
a thick of auburn hair;
Lips kissing collarbone...

The smell—suntan lotion,
A splash of chlorinated water,
a dash of Shalimar behind the ears from the night before,
And the sweat of hard-earned,
Heart-burned,
Maternal love.

Gasps and squeals and giggles;
More splashes of icy drops
soothing sun-baked skin.
Savouring life
Buoyed by heaving breathing breasts;
My human lifesaver.

It is the one thing...
One memory,
That can break the dam
That no lip-biting can abate
I'm free back then,
I think I'm three again...
Gasping; Clasping; Steadying; Readying;
then diving away into my first swim,
Slowly sinking into a sensory tsunami...
Then breaking the surface
of the watery memory;
reducing my eyes
to a swimming
pool of tears.

THE NIGHT OF THE FALLING STARS
(AN OICHE DO NA RÉALTAÍ AG TITIM)

for Mac and our magical times in Éire

I am trying to catch you,
Some of you, for parts of me...
As you dance across the constellation;
So I offer a Prayer for Love and Writing,
and the Muse who floats between the two.

Bursts of fire falling across the inky *Inis Mór* sky
Perseus has unleashed all of you, his progenies
Scattering you around the night heavens,
And I, hoping to catch you in twos...or threes,
pray for *mo anam cara* and some cosmic fire,
To ignite my imagination.

Am I needy or greedy? Or both?
And if I am, it's because you feed me,
I have it all with you, my holy Celtic trinity—
my soul's Claddagh ring;
cairdeas—the friendship, you dear muse, provide me
dilseacht—the loyalty I have for my words and they for me
gra`—the love that dares to speak his name,
and dares me to write it.

As I sit here, amidst these rocky ancestral cliffs
and sacred coastal soil,
bleeding ink, gasping for paper breath
These words are my laughing at death;
Praying for your stellar inspiration to
Give way to some enchanted respiration,
O, falling stars, I want to hold your fire,
Fill myself with your light...
So I can love better, so my mind can fly,
better able to write.
This is my mission, my curse, my destiny...
To see you soaring, to find you falling

Catching your elusiveness with both hands,
Making love that makes love new and possible;
And, if music is what language hopes to be,
Then I pray my words will sing to you softly;
And every moment a worthy thought, or consummation
signed in soul-blood, and
Each thought, if it be a pulsing one,
a prayer
to commit, fearlessly—to write, relentlessly
Of the loving flood, and
the only air.

THE BELFAST BOY AND THE NIGHT

for that wild Irish summer of '97

Such a woebegone little boy you are,
In need of peace, you bolt and take flight;
I wait, making sure you don't wander far.

Though you want me, you snip and spar,
Sometimes sweet, or ready for a fight;
Such a woebegone little boy you are.

Leaving your footprint on the windshield of my car,
Barefoot and freedom seeking, day or night;
I wait, making sure you don't wander far.

Teaching each other over whiskey at the bar
(The boy is smart, too), I lose my sober sight;
Such a sad, scared little boy you are.

Your sparks of laughter make you a blue star,
Changing before my eyes, man not quite;
I wait, making sure you don't wander far.

Like a fire-fly caught in the heart's glass jar,
Hard to hold, the burning power of your Gaelic light.
Such a woebegone little boy you are;
I'll still wait, making sure you don't wander far.

THE COLD THAT NEVER WENT AWAY

You had a cold that never went away.

I curled up beside you in your big mahogany bed,
that seemed smaller to me at 37.
Something I hadn't done in two decades...everything, even you,
looked smaller, faded and—
fading...
You, stoic Irish woman—*"Never sick a day in my life"*
I'm thinking now—and was then, too—
of your ability to save the day with gestures small and heroic,
as you built the foundation of my life.

But now...
Now, so sad. Now, so tired.
Your big, della Robbia blue eyes—glassy with exhaustion—
held the ebbing hope of our family
for so long.
We snuggled, face to face...you put an emaciated arm on my shoulder
like an injured loyal dog
My best friend;
"Are you OK, Mama?" My raspy voice, usually booming,
now breaking soft and gentle.
"Fine." Your unconvincing reply revealed a glimpse of the ugly
and immediate future.
"Are you...happy?" you asked with a fierce determination,
you usually reserved for moments
of terrifying truth.
"You're sick, Ma...how could I be happy?"

Sincerity wrestled with naïveté
and together they subdued my awareness that this was
a much bigger question.
"I want you to be *happy*; I need to know that he loves you
and you love him.
And, that you'll be alright."

Her thoughts fell from her mind to her mouth
with the keenness they always did.

"I *am*, Ma."

Your last lucid moment,
Even in that, you gave me something—a piece of you,
That never went away.

BLUE SNOW

Put away the pretty, little, bright-colored lights
Pack up the glittering, stars, ornaments and tinsel.
Quiet darkness is fitting for these icy
Bleak, blackish-gray December nights.

Throw out the stockings, tinsel and garland, too
It's numbing tonight, blue snow falls outside,
With fire-tears, I warm my lonely hands and
I whisper to myself: "Christmas died with you."

She left us silently beside the fireplace, where the tree,
Gloriously adorned every Season once stood.
And she, by the doorway, would lovingly hover and dote,
Proudly welcoming guests with smiling drinks warmly.

Those merry traditions are only memories now, true;
Our future seems impossible, the snow outside improbably blue.
With fire-tears, I warm my sad, lonely hands again, and
Whisper plainly to myself: "Christmas died with you."

THE TRAPEZE OF HOPE

On the way to the hospital it occurs to me:
you are not always going to be here,
Or there, where I've counted on you being for so many years.
Or ...
Now my mind gets stuck like the dust encrusted on the skipping cd
flicking and clicking on the car stereo,
I cannot think and drive,
I cannot think and drive well
At the same time,
I cannot think of losing you and drive...at all.
You ask, "where do we go?"
The truth is I have no vision;
and the cacophony of you, me and the skipping song
makes the emergent situation seem comical.
We find our way, groping and hoping through the automatic doors,
gliding across the waxed floors to the room
where you will be sliced open;

Like a valet undressing his gentleman,
delicately, quietly I remove your clothes.
You stare vacantly into my thoughts;
I slip you into the hospital gown with that unspoken tenderness
comprised of terror and devotion, forged by years of everything.

They wheel you away on the gurney;
You glide through the sea of white.
And my life freezes for a few hours of nothing.
The minutes pass; furious drops of eternity ebbing away
I become a pathetic, frenetic, peripatetic, skeptic
Who's more apoplectic than sympathetic;
I want to scream as I'm wandering the halls,
pondering the infinite illnesses and endless pains
pulsing throughout these corridors,
waiting for that call,
so I can take you home.

With fevered concentration, I study the linoleum
And analyze the contours of a paper coffee cup.
My mind drifts, enjoying the hallucinatory moments
Of memory and aspiration; unable to unravel what's happened,
what is happening and will happen next—or...eventually.
I find myself singing, pacing, and clinging to my
Italian sense of *speranza*;
Counting on a wee bit of my
Irish luck—or my mother Mary's words of wisdom
Coming to me.

But, for now, I just want "*now*" back;
and so I'm asking myself "*how*?"
The trapeze act of desire, swinging from memory to hope
from "was" to "will be"
And for a while longer I precariously dangle
from "*we'll see...*"

MEMORY'S SHADOW

for Bruce (Zio) Smith

Not the days
Not the hours
Not nearly

It is those moments of reflection—memory's reaching repose
When we spin through time
    —the velvety touch of the bedspread
    Stretched across the time of toddler to
    Tracing my finger in the curling and unfurling embroidered flowers
    Unaware that time was passing us by
The nurturing negative space in those lovely lost hours

Then it is the chaotic kitchen moments that make my mitral valve prolapse
Lapse and send me into a famished folly of trying to recall the recipes'
slightest details
    —the way she moved in such a small space
    Pouring out bowls full of happiness
    with such measured grace
    Made by delicate, freckled Irish hands, like the pasta
    that happily hangs from the towel rack,

These things I miss dearly, memories that cut nearly
I think to remember them more clearly, but they are but
brightly colored shadows—
Antiqued mirrors refracting something other than what
is being looked for—
Like a Benarcik print or Papaleo painting,
depicting something so truthful
but too honest to be life-like
or like life...

THE WAKE TOO SOON

in memory of David Westra

...too much sorrow
consumes the air
at the too soon
wake;
So heaving chests
attempt to hide
the suffocating
hearts.
Too much sorrow
consumes the air
at the too soon
wake.
So histories fall
from arid mouths
hoping to ease
minds;
too much sorrow
consumes the air
at the too soon
wake.

Too soon, too soon, too soon.

As our tongues grapple
with the ineluctable;
the unimaginable that
we need not imagine any longer—
the unendurable that
we are somehow enduring—
So that only
thoughts, not words,
have any room
to breathe.

CONSTANT INTERCESSION

She sat beside him,
Wrapped in her black and whites.
His broad shoulders stretched the funereal fabric
Hunched in an act of contrition.
Her gray hair, not too wavy to raise suspicions;
She was married to God, after all.
But so was he, which made it all the more confusing,
did that mean also
he was married to Him? And,
We all know the view was dim
On that subject.

But they were a comforting team together,
Father Tim and Sister Claire.
He, like Him, and she, like the Saint from Assisi,
Created a prickly pair;
Exuding an auspicious air and hiding their
Hidden spark—it wasn't easy.

The two would work the wakes and funeral masses,
Doling out platitudes and gratitudes generously
if not a bit too sincerely and dearly—
as if they had clearly
practiced long hours together.

This bright night at the funeral home
Brought the four back into
A common trajectory
But only for a dour hour.

The boys were such an odd pairing
Daring, that's true, for in those parts
Buddies didn't get too
Close, distance was a friend.
And this rather un-poetic duo's rhyme scheme was off:
Jack moved to a city
Jason stayed a local boy...
People still remembered their hi-jinx and high passes
on the field or in the hallways

Their curious connection
—as seductive as it was exclusionary;
Boys and girls were equally jealous—
If not a tad overzealous to be in their company.
Brick and Skipper had nothing on them, and evidence
Was sparse, save for the one summer when a single Jason
Had the confirmation of love's cruelly kind marks
Trailing across his neck
—like a purple version of the white
encircling Father Tim's collar—
Words spread like thickly spilled ink
but Jack was off to New York where he could hide
In the oblivion of obviousness;
Where all is so visible as to be hidden.

And those two boys whose shared past,
And not-so-different present,
kept them coming into each other's orbit,
And managed to balance the awkward rhyme
Scheme
Of the love they could never tame;
Of two different meters and with separate paces
And four faces;
Of a love that did not yet dare to speak
Its shame.

But every few years the passing of someone
would draw them back and take them off track
—or put them back on?
Falling through death's trapdoor
Into each other's arms...
Giving praise to the heavenly, while taking comfort
in the terrestrial consolation of flesh
        in a car's backseat,
        on a motel room floor.
They would, in their Sunday best,
Always stay until the end to show respect
And they would get into separate cars
Drive out to some of the bars

—Or the empty high school parking lot—
And drink and until the moon had set
High in the low New England sky
And let them be.
When they got good and drunk,
When their minds finished racing
and their inhibitions had sunk,
they would retire to the back seat
of Jason's truck or Jack's car
(Just like Father Tim and Sister Claire);
these so-called abominations:
     A sister and a father,
     A man lying down with another man;
They each said silent prayers
as their hearts ran, galloped toward ecstasy
in some way or another; praying just long enough for the
Endlessness of their moments
And the ending of their emotions.
None of which ever came
Or stopped coming.

Heroic couplets
In their own way, their smart rhyme unheard
And unseen—
All four of them that is,
—A random but consistent chance
At grace dropped into their hands;
The passing of another
has endowed their being lovers
for the briefest of times, again
—gifts of irretrievable, rapturous
stolen moments—
Through these countless crushing concessions...
And, always (all four of them) praying for
Deliverance from their Catholic fate,
And the Lord's
Constant Intercession

RUNNING AWAY

for Mary Cronin

On my 11th birthday
I ran away from home
maybe to find, but more to see—
I fled down the street,
walking and why-ing myself,
marching in my bare feet
along Route 9-A
toward Hastings, like William the Conqueror,
wondering if the battle was still raging that June.
But it was only just my hormones;
the testosterone turbulence
engaged in a duplicitous battle, fighting for
and on both sides...
leaving me unable to comprehend
my brother's need to leave;
that the sudden absence of Edward My Confessor
—14 now and high school bound—
created all that chaos and nothingness
in my little universe;
the third of three is such a blessing and a curse.

My mother soon pulled alongside me,
Gliding in her silver Skylark.
Matching my marching gait
She asked me to get in and talk.
I did.
She said: "People run away because they feel trapped
or invisible."
She paused with a heavy serenity,
that gave me everything that time and grace,
heaven and space, would allow;
"Which way do you feel?"

"I don't know." I lied.
—Afraid to bare a soul I was just discovering

and could hardly bear—
"Both…"

She smiled, understanding the nuance of my incoherence
and said: "Me, too, sometimes. But if you ran away,
I would miss you very, very much…"

She had that knowing half-smile;
That somehow reassured and left her
whole heart open
To a puckish chuckle or perfectly timed embrace.
Her profile split in my favor,
strawberry mane swirled away in a bun
(with a turquoise Navajo hairpin)
to reveal those blue storm-windows
One eye on the road, the other one,
on my soul.
Sensing my severity, she lit up a True Blue
        Inhaling her heavy thoughts and mine…
Hers: of her three lost sons; each with a faded name,
                None of whom ever reached one.
Mine: of my lyrical loneliness which somehow left me wordless,
                Searching for what's lost on the run.
And then exhaling…wisdom and smoke:
"You're *my* baby,
If you ran away, it would break my heart."

At the time, I did not quite comprehend
How much I (and the world) needed her;
How much depended on her indomitable spirit
—which was so much more affectionate inferno
than quiet fire—
How safe and cared for we all were
How she embodied everything Irish I knew—
Soul, grit, wit, and tenderness…

And now the *hummm* of a slowly passing car

creeping by a curb
or the sight of a lost boy following his heart
—or being followed—
breaks mine.

I crack at the smell of a remembered sweetness
—the incense of my youth—
so intense, so true;
One that only Mommy could imbue:
>   the confinement only she could liberate,
>   the loneliness she alone could keep company,
>   the invisibility only she could make seen,
>   the unending ache she so easily could attenuate.

These days,
Despite the many innovations in transportation,
No one can
Bring me back...
So
My mind keeps
Running away.

LIKE ÉIRE

for Pamela Rader

I want to be you
I want to be like you
I want to be more like you

I want to breathe your air

Floating
           In motion;
                      Autonomous,
Shifting and still
So still the world revolves around you—
Answering to no one
In your own orbit
both earth and sun;

O, Island
O, I-land
To be unto yourself
So sufficient,
           Alone
                      I want to be part of you
Your sand and grass and stone

Untouchable;
Often unreachable
Trusting the of protection of the sea
Relishing the safety of your daunting distance
Your illuminating isolation defines free

(isle, isla, isola...isolato)

You,
So mysterious
With your layers of antiquity;
O, what your centuries have

Meant to me; trying to know you
More deeply
Your craggy coastline
Filled with inlets and coves
Aging secrets like wine
or whiskey
in ancient the casks
of improbable tomorrows

Now, I see your two peninsulas
Flanked on each side
Like arms outstretched
Indefinitely waiting for
An infinite embrace,
Or
Infinitely waiting for
An indefinite embrace

       Yet, definitely waiting for a definite embrace
like me

(isle, inis, oileán, ina-aonar)

O, Island
O, I-land
I want to be you,
I want to be like you,
I want to be more like you
       (I want to be like Éire)
Maybe, I am

FLOWER THIRST

My
    Love
       Is
          Skyborne
             Water
               Droplets
                  Falling
`
                     Onto
                     The
                  Hungry
              Earth
          To
      Quench
    Your
  Flower
Thirst.

SEEING HER EYES, SOMETIMES NEVER

(after E. E. Cummings)

i can't even say why i **miss** you so much, and, so often;
the living-loss of the soothing caress of **your** daily **smiles**
that were deeper than any glen's green? not even the wild
blue Malin Bay has such **fierce** and understanding **eyes**

ANAM CHAIRDE

for my Celtic Culture Club Children

Born, am I,
Of clan McCann
>   —from Lough Neagh
>   over Blackwater
>   down the River Bann—
Mac Cana (Son of the Wolf Cub)
Heirs to kings and lords and warriors
>   —an ancient, intricate, infinite
>   Irish bloodline—

A shared transcendent descendancy

And you, my cub,
>   —in this other world
>   across the wanton,
>   wanting Atlantic—
Are, indeed, my son, my daughter
My soul's friend (*mo anam chara*)
T'was the twisting, turning roads
>   that made you mine.

Part II

Cuore Spudorato
Chroí Gan Náire
Shameless Heart

"Tutto il problema della vita è dunque questo: come rompere la propria solitudine,
come comunicare con altri...
Non si ricordano i giorni, si ricordano gli attimi."

"The whole problem of life, then, is this: how to break out of one's own loneliness,
how to communicate with others...
We do not remember days; we remember moments."

—Cesare Pavese, *"Il Mestiere di Vivere"*

"Basta scavare in ogni piccolo fatto e diventa una miniera.
Il banale non esiste. Ogni momento è infinitamente ricco."

"It is enough to excavate every small thing and become a miner of life.
Banality doesn't exist. Every moment is infinitely rich."

—Cesare Zavattini, *"Il Banale Non Esiste"*

"Wishing with All His Might" Copyright Susan Benarcik ©2020

LISTENING TO DYLAN

for Bob Dylan, Seamus Heaney, and my Papà

My Italian father is listening to Dylan, again.
        He misses her.
        He misses his old life.
The door to his room is locked, I never
know what that might mean.
I don't know why it makes me so
sad.
He's become a "Mr. Tambourine Man" at 88
And we're both jingle-jangling
       —he from the various medications,
his unsteady gait from neuropathy—which sounds like something good
but isn't.
       —me from the cacophony of coughs and sighs,
the dope of mixed emotions and memories he reluctantly sells me;
That uncertain ending he's pushing.
                (Which makes me the addict;
                the son's always the addict.)

I am staying with him;
             (And he with me.)
He locks the doors at night...
afraid.
Old people scare easily but fear little;
a workable conundrum that comes
with cataracts and cancer scares.

It's the sudden things that take everything away;
the never-ending news feeds—that torturous diversion
that ravages the aging spirit;
Or the endless phone calls announcing the fateful fading away
of friends and relations; that loneliness
that dare not speak its name;
to do so might welcome the great exile itself.
No sudden movements, please.
           It's the sudden things that take everything away...

He doesn't fear much, just further loss.

Now, I am listening to Dylan, too
I am here, and though it is the house
I have known all my life, I'm lost...
utterly lost
in it...
it's unfamiliar,
un-familial, since Ma died.

I make his meals. I cook and clean
and try to make things normal...
                             (like before?)
I cook and write poetry, in a room I slept in as a teenager
I write poetry he is reluctantly proud of,
and I am left fearing the success I almost had at 34.

I don't know how long I can stay or should or will,
it's as hard to say as it is to see;
I'm like Blanche DuBois, "just passing through"
I hope I meet a better end than she.
I think Orpheus once asked in a song: "Are we all born in our lonely skins,
destined to spend our lives alone in them?"
                             (But even I, now, can't believe
                             such a sad thing is true.)

                           It's the sudden things that take everything
                           away...
He fears being alone; he "hates it," he says
When he's alone, he keeps asking himself questions,
How many times must a man?...
but he just can't find the answers...
they're "Blowing In The Wind"—the next song I hear,
And everything good seems...blown away.
                           He misses her.
                           He misses his old life.
So, I am listening to Bob Dylan, again, too.

And, I remember snowbound weeks in our little ski cabin
fire-cracking with personalities; my aunts and uncles and
cousins and Grandma Grace—we packed ourselves into
our frosty paradise of perfect moments of contentment...
and nothing mattered at all because all that mattered was there.
We sang and told stories by the fire and no one got old;
my aunt Margaret and mother, Mary, in the kitchen, glasses of wine in one
      hand,
wooden spoons in the other, swaying to the beat,
"Forever Young" and laughing just like little girls,
and making the impossible a riotously recollectable reality
—more than the meals of the moment but the food of memory, safe from
      decay.
Like Rolling Stones with no direction known, the big boys
wax their skis and read sports magazines and dream of better skiing in
Utah and Colorado...
The big girls dote on me, the baby boy, and we begin what will be
the first of life-saving, life-long conversations.
After dinner, around the fire...Uncle Jack and Uncle Jimmy
Would strum their guitars with a fervent effortlessness,
               —that we Irish do so well—
They'd sing like Bobby Dylan—they called him "Bobby" like they knew him.
Like he was one of us,
On those snowy evenings of my 1970s youth
where my whole happiness
was found in the coziness of our Celtic Clan
in the laughter of my cousins and
belonging...
            (maybe the other Bobby—Sands—was right,
            our laughter *is* the revenge of our ancestors?)
The mournful melodies of Dylan's harmonica,
his Cassandra-like, warbling warnings,
            "The Times They Are A Changin'"—
Times change, memories don't—
            It's the sudden things that take everything
            away...
And they were.

And we didn't even know it—years passed, like bullets shot underwater
And now, Papa sits in his hurricane of loneliness, staring off at the skylla
      of sorrows
keening into the kharybdis of regrets...
absorbed now, again, in Dylan, he's trying to find something,
a moment of a memory...?
It's my job to pull him back—I was a lifeguard—

                        (for five summers, back when I was
                        someone I knew;
                        But I take solace in Wilde's quip;
                        "Only the shallow know themselves,"
                        which rings too true)

I am rescuing the drowned again, but it's a different kind of drowning—
Memories that keep him afloat shift to stones
And I wonder what he's thinking as he's all
"Tangled Up in Blue"?

                        He misses her.
                        He misses his old life.

I sit, dreaming, it's not a job for most, but this house is a house of dreams,
      now.
I sit in the middle of it all, dreaming;
lost again, but certain my memories matter.

                        It's the sudden things that take everything
                        away...
                        (like getting older)

And for a few seconds it was 1976, the tumult of the 60s' storms had passed...
No escape.
No one escapes.
But for us, it will soon start to fall apart

                        (Now, Yeats is telling me "the center cannot
                        hold")
                        It's the sudden things that take everything
                        away...
He asks, "Oh, where have you been, my blue-eyed son?"

And I can't tell him, I never could—
The snow has turned now...and it's "A Hard Rain's Gonna Fall"
40 years later—there's less pleasure and more pain.
He's listening to Dylan again,
"Just Like A Woman"—
and I surprise myself as I laugh when I hear
"nobody feels pain."
He's in his locked room, again,
dreaming of his widow, his woman
His Queen Mary...
His lovely Irish lass, his beautiful past,

> He misses her. Mary.
> He misses his old life.
> It's the sudden things that take everything
> away...
> (Like getting older...
> ...like losing your wife
> ...like passion's glorious pain
> ...like losing part of your life)

My eyes burn with the pitiless uncertainty of what's left—
Of both our lives,
We're all tangled up in a messy and murky,
brackish-blue something,
In my head I hear, Dylan croon: "If Not For You"

> He misses her, again.
> He misses his old life;
> His lost wife.
> And, I do too...

LOSING ITALIA

for Raffaele Ronca

Random, peculiar,
how it swiftly hits you;
Walking down Fifth Avenue through the arches
at Washington Square Park
The who-why-when-what-where-how...smacks me—
'no schiaffo across the face
like the women in my family would do
when at their wit's middle;
(I think I'm there now,
stuck in the endless in between)
Years of thinking with only half of an American brain
Speaking with a forked tongue will do that;
Makes you feel like a lost fraud; unsure of your next step
as much as your last word;
either way you're stumbling toward
another inopportune epiphany.

So I start to question why I am even here, now.
Mumbling quietly, sad supplications to myself
I ask: Why do I long for a day
Or night
'na giornata or 'na serata, doesn't matter:
a time—a place—a memory
that gives me the peace, the harmony
I once felt for not long enough,
Not too long ago?

When I sat in the *Campo de' Fiori*
drinking the sun,
perhaps becoming one
with my espresso,
feeling—belonging—
living each day part of a vibrantly ancient bloodline
every evening feeling that somehow Italia
was mine.

Where the time is deliberate—
and the people serene in their warmth
surrounded by those subdued colors:
terracotta, gesso, pietra
words that make love to your tongue
parole che fanno l'amore con la lingua...

Italian days are designed and built;
Constructed for connection,
Via, Piazza and Passeggiata demand it;
In the land of eternal yesterdays the now is all
and no little thing incidental,
Not a church bell wasted on regrets and recriminations:
The message muttered from the ancestral dead
Is to not just politely exist;
But to live *(Viva!!!)* with exclamations—
for in Italia *'na chiacchierata*—even with the long gone
is simply impossible to resist.

What matters is the soul—*"bell'anima"*
the face is but a frame;
eyes that tell—hands that speak
words that feel unabashedly
with songs and cries!
A certain pride in their—our?
Unbridled *passione*.

But *here* they tell me to always calm down;
(Passione sfrenata...) no brakes on the passion, please!
"Don't be so animated" they try to convince me.
I try to tell "them": brakes are for cars
Not for the ectoplasm of Eros that pulses non-stop
through your body, like the flight from JFK to DaVinci.

Why isn't it the same here?
To myself I'm talking as I'm stalking down
5th Avenue amongst the walking dead;

Checked out hipsters and the gloomerous illiterati;
Pill popping poseurs and anti-socialites
with their faces pulled tight;
Why? (I am back to 'why,' again?)
The faded plaster and stone walls along the *Via della Maschera d'Oro*
Have slightly more expression and infinitely more to say.
A façade is just that, a face.
But, here, the external reigns supreme
and always wins the race.
But, I'm out of the running or
Simply losing steam
living my American life
with one foot just off Broadway,
the other in a neo-realist dream.

How I want to return...to the land of many ands
Always more...*ancora*—
To go away from these cold people,
this vague climate;
Through another set of arches,
The Arco Tito, maybe, and glide
Caesar-like among the
Foro Antico, and slide and glide
Passing the past, running my hands along
The cool sooty stone of the *Colosseo;*
And, yet again, I want to find myself
and discover and roam,
like I just stepped out
of *La Dolce Vita,*
into a land that
calls my blood
home.

THE RETURNING IMMIGRANT

for Nonna e Pisticci—Prov. di Matera

Papà, I am leaving
> *Sì, sì, ci voglio andare*
don't ask why
you already know
and have hid it from yourself
for so long
blinding you—burning in your ears
for an eternity
those cold hopes—last breaths—lost years
gasping words—grasping for *la terra natia*
held prisoner in her throat:
> *"Nun lasseme morì ca…Ijë nun vojo morì ca"*
> *(don't let me die here…I don't want to die here)*
ever resounding
forever startling
your eerie daydream moments
your tormented, scream-filled awakenings
quiet disturbances—that never let you rest
an unfulfilled promise you let slip away
broken like a statue from antiquity
lingering like graveyard mist
a distant touch—a solitary love
buried in a foreign land,
Here,
haunted still

I went back to Italy,
So *she* could rest in peace.
And, now, Papà,
> *O mio babbino caro*
I really must go…again
> *Sì, sì, ci devo tornare*

I will see you on the
Other side

Where we can breathe our
ancestor's *aria Lucana* together
and give *Nonna*
Un giusto addio—a proper good-bye.

THE STORGE SOLUTION

for H. J. P.

The teacher stood at the front of the classroom,
Like Cicero watching the gathering hungry,
Hormonal barbarians,
Looking for someone
He didn't yet know.

He then opened the door (hopeful and cautious)
For a countless, timely time
And let the already late boy
—who roamed about like La Lupa's lost wolf pup—
In.

Stalking and stumbling around the dense forest of drab desks,
His heavy backpack slung around strong shoulders,
a thick eyebrow arched, the boy-pup
Skulked and bobbed as he flip-flopped into the
Unfolding arms of the unknown.

Then their eyes leerily locked;
Who the hell is this guy?
The boy's thoughts grousingly growled.
This one's going to be trouble,
The teacher's mouth numbly mumbled.

And because of all that, the teacher seemed oddly intimidated
And strangely thrilled
To see this boy emerge from the dark, ancient Roman hills.
Whereas, the boy was simply there, perfectly
At home with his youthful insecurities, new-found freedoms,
And clever curiosities—
A wild problem child
He *hoped* to solve.

Like Odysseus readily recognizing his time-lost Telemachus,
They knew their souls knew each other.

It made no sense, after so many years,
Save for the fortuitous fact that
The classroom woodland teems with creative zeal,
(and boys like wolf pups are rare)
But, as Cicero said, *where there's life—there's hope.*
And it's in the filling, emptiness is revealed.

Their eyes would soon meet again, everything
  suddenly-slowly understood
They improbably belonged to each other;
The problem child—he was now *destined* to solve
  in four frenzied, fleeting years...

  The problem (the teacher learned)
  Was the solution,
  Part of a once lost longing;
  A certain *storge* revolution.

   And the reason it took me five years to write this
   —in notebooks, on cocktail napkins, and around test
   questions—
   is what I unknowingly felt was all quite real
   —the fear and pride and all the love in between—
   was only what a parent could feel.

TWO THINGS NOT ALLOWED
IN THIS ROOM

The clock is a machine that
Eats good and bad,
Equally with rapturous delight
Delectable, we are
The good ones...

I prostrate my poor psyche in fear of your
hovering hunger, which never comes...

Unlike the clocks, the mirrors
only consume the bad,
They never have much appetite
but for their own vanity;
I avoid the merciless, unflinching stare as
I dart and dash about
trying not to see me...

They are bad, too, the mirrors: narcissistic cannibals.
Clocks and Mirrors; I hate them both.
Like vigilant vampires—Sucking your blood-time
and showing you the horrific process all the while.

Then, what are the good things?
Surely not the cacophonous television;
spewing its prurience and paranoia,
Perhaps, then, the telephone? the computer?
Gracelessly redirecting—without connecting—
our emotions and voices through the infinity of space?
These bookshelves surrounding me—are they good?
Hmmmm...they are *always* there for me;
Sturdy in studiousness, constructed for consistency
and loyal in oaken luminosity;
shelves filled with many paths and singular truths...
Demanding only one thing: engagement, thoroughly;
that sounds 'good' to me.

Through this symbolic symbiosis,
I look for the proof in these syllogistic spoofs
and make conclusions that turn in on themselves,
and offer me pretty unanswerable questions.

       No! Basta!
       Go! Enough!

With time exiled and vanity vanquished,
I look around this room;
built of a billion words and
Buckets of ink, the blood spilled on the battlefield of blank paper.
Life betraying Death with her bliss-filled kiss—
Where *then* and *now* peacefully coexist,
on the pages packed and stacked all about,
and I tussle and scuffle trying to work
this poem out.

SEA, LIFE

for Susan Benarcik

We are each of us
magnificent
sailing vessels:
our bow filled with unexpressed desires;
our stern weighted with the anchors
of dashed dreams.

Our flags fly high,
Flapping and snapping,
declaring our allegiance
to our completeness? Or
to the endlessness of the oceanic whirrr—

...that seductive sound whose pulse creates
a fundamental fury;
Tack or jibe, the choice is ours
Seeking psychic healing through
our solid keel and soaring heeling

The *vento* is ever precarious,
Predictably unpredictable; gusts or gales
        (as Zefiro is wont to blow)
And, yet, it is all that our headsails
can rely upon...
We're just built that way.

        And sometimes during
        those moments when we bother to listen
        and stop simply enduring...
        We hear Seneca whisper: "If one does not know
        to which port one is sailing, no wind is favorable."

And so we are blown about by windy want,
We chant and scream; we prostrate and dance,
Through fated straits, on unforeseen seas

Piercing the sky with our inaudible pleas
in leaving we forget everything to chance.

So we pray the mast will last
And keep us upright and strong,
We can go on...Can we go on?
Trying to hold on to our stays;
So that we do not unravel too fast...

We spend most of our time alone—
confinement amidst a vast and
vacillating sea;
succumbing to ponderous undulations
that take us nowhere.
Or worse, where we're not wanted
And no longer want to be...

We go searching for that dimming light
that reaches out
in the expanding hole of darkness,
fighting for peace and
seeking a companion soul
for some piece of this puzzling journey.

And always ever hoping our direction is correct,
And that we will have somehow
Earned high station;
But only vaguely certain,
whether desired or dreaded,
of our own destination
—the soul's *terra firma*

CHIARO/SCURO

The summer I watched the grapevine grow
was the summer
I lost my innocence

Every day and into the night...
I sat watching the grapevine grow
Twining, pining, and vining around the lattice arbor

They both called on me that summer, and I eagerly followed
Showing me the red and white of life, I plunged headfirst
Drowning my thirst in
Rosso passion and *Bianco* desire swept me away
to a land of no choices
The grapes grew side by side

The fiery, sun rose and set, day after day,
beaming through the shield-like grape leaves
Apollo's blaze ripened the virgin grapes, and bathed me in its warmth,
strength, and power.
I studied him with burning admiration,
as he taught me vigorously

Until the moon came. And she, cool and white,
surprised me every night,
by grabbing my heart as she shone through the lattice of the arbor.
In perfect darkness she alone was luminous. And I watched her with the
sweetest devotion while she caressed me deeply, to sleep.

The smooth essence drifting down my waiting throat,
kept my thirst quenched, but left me always wanting
for another sunset or sunrise.

Il Fratello Sole and *La Sorella Luna*
awakened all my senses
Tasting each grape, different from the other,
Savored and then known...

The summer I watched the grapevine grow,
The summer I lost my innocence,

The summer I fell and soared

It was the summer I let myself be
Seduced by *Chianti's rosso* and *Vernaccia's bianco*...
And in those days and nights I learned
to drink from two glasses
raising one
to the Sun
and one
to the Moon.

EDGE OF BED

I like to sleep on the edge;
where I find myself calling, falling,
Enthralling;
All through the towering power
of the small hours...
Laying on the edge allows me to ride and
slide down these mean sheets, and confide
in my pillows; arms weeping over the bed's edge
like wanderlustful willows,
touching the world of reason below that I know awaits me,
but it will have to wait for me. It's a hunger
for gravity and speed
and knowing how it will feed my mind
when Incubi and Succubae do battle in my head,
boy, it's a crowded bed...
with no room for Morpheus and his tender arms.
This orgy of memories and missed opportunities—
lies and desires;
found sorrows and lost tomorrows—leaves me playing
with hidden fires;
there is so much to be done under the covers
and in my eyes' rapid movements...the waking climax
is soaking hot like an open mouth kiss...
In those moments, the torrents wildly run
from ecstasy to dread.
The mutating montage in my motionless fury
while above my head
hangs a sword of Damocles;
want, regret, dissatisfaction, inadequacy—
my battles with thieves
offers no peace, and only insomnia would ease the welling
and swelling and my constant dwelling...
and offer some control in consciousness.

I need to sleep on the edge...
Once awake I attempt to make sense;
and in creeps the pretense of the analytical mind.

Battling the reasonings that spring after
these nocturnal transmissions:
Feel free to flee, waking still, more,
there is another attempt at smashing the dawn;
or is it some old dream
of my heart, half in shadow, as it crosses
the unspeakable line?

Maybe I was just dreaming on the edge at the
end of the world,
drifting toward a new horizon; where the sea is having
a threesome with the earth and sky;
and my pleading greedy hardness points me
up into some right direction...

Somehow, slowly and startlingly,
through my own irrelevance
I begin to make sense; awakening—in some way—
estranged from myself,
My strange self, but
Embracing the distance
with one foot on the floor,
Still grounded in my very real imagination,
which is a great substitute
for the other alternative.

KIND WAVES   1

for Newport in August

I come to watch your graceful inevitability, which reminds me
I am nothing,
kindly,
such truths must always be delivered, delicately your heaving
is reassuring—like the resting of an anguished head
on a mother's breast—longed for by a no-longer boy
years and miles apart, your vastness separates and propitiates
my longing in its swirliness

The rhythm of aquatic undulations, (a certain mathematical calmness)
Sets me to thinking of something that feels a lot like nothing.
The salt helps, too...it always does—in all its symbolic splendor
Heaven's lachrymose deposits.

I watch, and I breathe, far
from the suffocating city,

                                    Cities are designed to be
                                    escaped from

—like prisons people try to break into

For now, I am lost in your infinite blue   Your comings and goings
                                                  suited for a quixotic lover
Each one of you, a stranger

                                                  Whose kindness I always
                                                  depended on;
And as long as I sit here, we are and will be...
A 21st century Neruda, a contented exile drawing water,
Drawing from your water; the desire to continue
by simply stopping,
at least for a while...

INKY WAVES OF DESIRE   II

for those Italian summers

Your constancy,

Unyielding and inevitable,

Wet like a silvery want;

Unable to be man-handled

Or even held...briefly.

You own me;

Incapable island that I am,

Surrounded,
By natural hazards that are inescapable...

By day you caress me,

Stroke and stoke me;

Changing my form with the protean power
Of your amorphousness;

Altering my content at your
Relentless will.

On occasion, your wanton wanting

Brings hurricane pains that
Grip and rip

And strip me to my muddy sandbar core;
But I am resilient alone with my words.

At night, you are more subtle

With your surreptitious
splashing—your languid
lapping

Stealthily beating down my resistance...

A thirst whose desire and
Satiation diametrically
increase

With your salty wetness.

But the moon controls you as much as
She haunts me
Using those forces, like a million wild horses;
Pushing and pulling me to write

                                        Or make love, or
Write and make love...

The ecstasy of a consummated burst of words
                                        Pumping out of me,

Your taunting leaves me wan and wanting   (an inverted island deserted)

I want to lick a page or a neck   Stroke and suck the life

Out of an idea, out of some-thing or some-one...

Again, I take a naked stand, with nothing
But my meager,   -
Eager pen in my hand.

ROMA MIA

It is hard, sometimes, to see you
Squinting eyes, walking the *Foro Antico,*
Combing piazzas, looking up—
Passing these bright, blue days...
Trying not to notice the pieces of you falling away,
Gazing upon your crumbling pieces of eternity.
Just lingering longer; enough to savor you.
But then, amongst your sea of discoveries,
I find I'm losing the ways to recognize you, again,
I don't know what is trickier; your face or my memory?
I slide down off the *Lungotevere* and hide out in the *Via Giulia*
Hoping you won't see me puzzling at your fading visage.
The gurgling fountains, your steady breath—
Remind me of the ancient times
I try to recapture in a gaze.

I want to see you again; the way you were,
Without the stultifying buzz of electricity.
You glow better by gaslight or a lantern's flame.
The great luminous beauty—unmarred by vapidity
This backward haze and these unforgiving days
Show the lines and ravages of modernity,
That bring you such undeserved shame.

The chariots have been replaced with *Vespas*
And the fiats that once fell from Caesar's mouth,
Today hum along your serpentine streets, blocking your veins.
I wander through you—feeling the pulse that has pumped—
All these centuries, hypnotized by its beat, contemplating the
       change.
But I cannot escape you...
These *vias* and *viales* are somehow still the same,
Still holding secrets filled with joy and pride and pain.

CRAWLING UP INTO ETERNITY
(OR IL COLOSSEO DI NOTTE)

for Lidia Vitale

Standing serenely sun-baked, exhausted yet imperious.
Or are you on one knee: a weary warrior,
The gallant gladiatrix seeking shade?
  'n core d'omo dintro 'na bella donna,
a man's heart in a beautiful woman

The day is not so kind to you,
But, night is consoling in its velvety veil.
The strokes of moonlight illumine a perfect arch,
   where an unknown god once stood;
welcoming me with its comforting curve,

And I could crawl up into eternity.

ANONYMOUS, BUT NOT TO ME

From the kitchen doorway,
through the portico of our alcove—
The arch of his bare foot cries vulnerability,
veins, smooth engravings winding up and down
Legs wrapped around the brocade sheets—
columns to my ancient Roman temple.

Shoulders flat across the bed,
flying buttresses, an impressive wingspan—
I want to climb atop and soar!
Taut lower-back, golden tan, dips and curves into a crevice—
two white mounds of marble are so inviting.
Generous arms reach out, crushing the pillows in his grasp—
Muffling a plea for my return?
Or is it Angry Love—
Antaeus to my Hercules...del Pollaiuolo's flailing entanglement,
begging for more of
some unspeakable
...something...

I glimpse pain and pleasure wrapped in white cotton—
The carved crease of a flexed tricep stirs my hunger.
The other lonely hand, open and hopeful, calling me—
Our abandoned desire, still waiting—
I am missing from that infinite embrace.

My bronze statue 'After Michelangelo',
Anonymous, but not to me.
His face captivates, remains hidden, forbidden;
I look back again, my eyes strain to see the fallen sculpture
—buried in a nebulous mound—
Kissing heaven, playing hard to give
in his early morning slumber.

My aching arousal doesn't stop me from making *caffè latte*
or pouring juice.
I grind and sizzle, coffee beans and bacon

—trying to cast a spell—
Feeling the distant hum of his resting body
Savoring the moments of our disrupted silence that
only early morning knows.
I rouse him to the breakfast table with a kiss
to his toes
        And only morning ever knows.

THAT ENDLESS NAME

"FRANCESCO MARIO D'ALESSANDRO"
Write it
Again, and again
Crying, at 7, struggling
To get all of those letters...Right...
Over and over again;
Why?—I thought—
Most people call me
'Frankie'
My Italian relatives call me *"Franchì"*
As a *bambino* I was *"Franchino"*
The *"bello biondino"*
And *"Ciccio"* was just a nickname
That my chubby ruddy cheeks made plain.
Hearing the bilingual echoes
of my name
Mutating
"Francesc"..."Fran-ghee"..."Fran-kee"...
Tears *tarantella*-ed down my face
Looking at my father's
Desperate, determined,
"Dago" eyes
And I realized; I assumed
his pain, I mean...name,
I—don't know what I mean...
Realizing his phonic frustration
Without understanding it,
Yet.

"Fr-a-a-nk!"
My mother would shout
(Pop married an Irish-American girl)
He was called *"Frank"*—now
He ditched and switched
To fit in;

My father, writhing in indecision,
My hand and pen quaking at the "N"
I am up to my neck in this
"What do I write next for this...
a C or a K?"
I already knew I'd lose
either way.
Then Pop would whisper the letters of my name—
And I would try to recover from the
Increasing sense of shame.

You see he had fathered
A 'Johnny' and an 'Eddie'
And I was his *'Francesco'*
Like a...fresco
His work of art,
His namesake,
His experiment,
To remake
His own trauma
To recreate
His own ancestry
La Storia, that was, now, slowly
Fading...the part of him
He chased—away and after—
Simultaneously.

Maybe, I thought,
They'd take their chances
With Francis,
But like the Saint I ain't,
Or was I?
I sure do love animals, and
With my wild-eyed
Sexual desires, the altered altar boy
danced between devotion and

playing the diligent dilettante,
I was a resolved child with a problem:
What to do? So much to do...
Over something as simple
And seismic as my name.

Nonna Pasqualina, who never learned English,
would roll her eyes;
Feeling foreign in front of her progeny
and thinking, *we are not this...This is not us!*
The protestations of a patrician peasant;
Nonna scolds: *"nun scordar' mai chi samo"*
(*never forget who we are*)
What sorts of frantic dances
in the ground
she must be doing now?

But then, finally,
Mom would plead: "Oh, leave him alone!"
Knowing of the right of initiation
Taking place in her American kitchen
Of the lie being uncovered
Of the ruins being unearthed
And it frightened her.
She loved the name Francesco;
(after all she married one)
To her the name was romantic;
At birth it was mellifluous,
Now, it was just...superfluous.

My older brothers chiming in:
"You can't call him that!"
"They'll think he's a sissy!"
"That's a girl's name!"
Mom out-shouted by her boys;
Pop defeated by Word War II

—his own moniker madness;
My horror at this chaotic chorus
Voicing and foisting
Persisting and insisting
that *"Frank"* was good enough.

And, please, lose the *'-cesco'*,
Far too ethnic!
I was apparently in need of
Some Medieval emergency surgery
To leach the Cheech out of me.

The boys win;
No more *Francesco!*
In an atmosphere so contentious,
Franco was just too pretentious for
A family fighting to fit in.

Over the years I felt
Pieces of me hacked away;
Forget about the middle M for *'Mario'*
(*My Irish granny still playfully whispers to me*
Frankie, the "M" really stands for McCreely)

Frank would be—to everyone but me who would wear it—
More acceptable,
More appropriate
More American
But this *more* made less of me.

And so *"Frankie"* went off to school
Surrounded by a swirl of American
Boys and girls;
And seeing his New World through the prism
Of Anglo-centrism.
The boy with the longest ethnic name;

The kid who always went home for lunch;
The one whose house smelled like garlic
and basil;
The wop whose house echoed with arias of Puccini;
The one who resisted feeling any shame
but tried so hard to be
Like everybody else.

But I was like an Italian super-hero,
whose secret identity
was his own ethnicity,
and whose only true lie
was forever masked in front of me.

In my teens I discovered
Fellini, DeSica and Rossellini
Magnani, Sofia and Mastroianni
I not only watched them
I felt as though they had seen me.
and later; Pavese, Pirandello,
Calvino, DeFillipo and Moravia...
The words did a *salta in bocca*
And I devoured them like the
endless montage of meals served in our home.
I was more, now,
than the *fettuccine alla carbonara,*
the *melanzane alla parmigiana* and the *lasagne alla bolognese*
That perfumed the streets of my neighborhood,
and garnered my friends' praise.
I was more than "The Godfather" movies,
And their parade of poor permutations
and the ensuing endless imitations.
A trans-Atlantic transfiguration occurred,
Stirring the sea within me,
A metaphysical communication between
Food, Culture and the Holy Ghost

As this profound connection was made.
My mind's earth broke new ground,
And as it pushed forth
the lie became truth.

I sadly realized that *Francesco*
Was washed up across the *Oceano Atlantico;*
Somewhere on the *Golfo di Taranto,*
or perhaps unborn, but somehow dead.
And he waits to be rescued,
Revived,
By having his name, finally, said.

Years later, no longer that boy
I found *Franco*
When I met myself and
Others who spoke my first,
Lost language.
I saw myself reflected
In those wondrous and wily words,
La lingua Italiana.
And sighed with a spirited relief
The comfort of a kissed pain
The dignity of a confirmed
Long-held belief.

So call me *Franco,* now
I am a reinvention
Of the real thing.
Francesco is a still born;
And *Frankie* died of SIDS,
he will forever live in memory
as that puckish little kid.
Frank has drowned in shallow waters
And drifted out to sea.
And I am left here and left behind

like some anthropomorphizing
De Chirico tree.
They are all dead now, all gone somehow.
And I've grown into the narrator,
who is merely, only, just me.

What to call me?

IO E LA NOTTE
(ME AND THE NIGHT)

We are companions;
the flirting stars don't matter, we both run from the day.

Your inky soul, black and blue—
reminds me of the pen not lifted, and the pristine pages.

And I run home at sunrise;
ready to write about the something we discovered...

Siamo compagni;
le stelle che flirtano non contano,
scappiamo entrambi due dal giorno.

La tua anima inchiostrata, blu e nera—
mi ricorda la penna non sollevata e le pagine immacolate.

E corro a casa all'alba;
pronto a scrivere qualcosa che
abbiamo scoperto insieme...

OUR HEARTS WERE WALLED CITIES

That long, swoony afternoon,
As we laid down on your broken-down bed,
and I think we heard time dancing an Irish jig in both our heads.
My fingers played with your toes, and your hands traced
the outline
of my Greco-Roman nose,
and I caressed your ears—worthy of a Roman emperor.
There...on the Posture-Pedic cloud of Eros, we were just friends—
there...where we lingered for hours
switching, head to head,
we wondered "how" this would end;
lips too close for discomfort as we half-dangled with our strewn bodies
across the white waves of cotton sheets of our island-spread.
No need for explanations,
no room for my ruminations, a poem in my head was born instead.

It was that soft and solemn day,
we granted each other access into our walled cities;
no Greek gifts or wooden horses needed.
A friendship forged in Roman blood and Celtic fire;
Each other's burdens we promised to carry,
Discovering such queer comfort
in sweetly sudden closeness.

MARINA'S CURSE

I've walked among the rock and ruin
   —Of a great moment,
I long to recognize my face
   —But reflections in shattered glass
   Do not compel me;
Solitary stultifying vision
   —Sisyphus to conformity,
I stay silent and I'm disappearing again
   —Drowning in the eternal
   Ebbs of men;
A wave in someone else's ocean
   —and I die every at sunrise...

And in the desolate evening, I fall again,
   —like Icarus back to the swallowing sea;
Awakening again, each day, to a whirling world
   —That commands me...
Able to imagine a distant dawn
   —One fine morning—
When I, having vanquished the stars,
Will speak louder, fly higher, reach farther,
And, win!

Oh, if I were Circe...

OUT OF PLACE

for Joseph Papaleo

i escaped to that undiscovered and hauntingly familial place
columns, terraces, fountains, porticos
seeking protection in marble, stone and brick
comforted by frescoes, walls that speak to me
the colors of an ancient spectrum: simplicity—duality—space

lingering lively chats at midnight
wondering walks through piazzas,
haunted...hoping...stealing pieces of time
living with a rare easiness;
sitting, patiently, sun-soaked,
traveling through centuries with the shift of an eye
learning newness in day's azure light

i will return to that now fading place
where people are the same as breezes:
capricious and kind, soothing and determined
where the beauty is not simply seen,
but touched, eaten and savored...
the soul's daily intoxication with grace

i have lost myself here—my ways
trying to find the beauty in exile
out of sync—out of place!
i have lost my way here—my *self*
fast food—fast love—fast life
i am left hungering for those lost days

i was born out of time—out of place
a Roman ruin of a life, glorious and fragmented
hoping to find *in motion what is lost in space*
i start to feel, i am losing again
gaining less with each year, more of me disappears
i close my eyes—making the sign of the cross,
another year—another thought

another meal—gaining more loss
      surviving is remembering, so
i remember to survive...

LIFE'S TORMENTED TANGO

I escorted Anna home, that last night...
hugs and kisses, hugs and kisses,
an air of not wanting the night to end, of holding on...
Anna waving and blowing kisses
                          "Ciao amore! Ciao caro, Ciao Tenn..."
She sauntered away, a lilt in her step that boasted
pride and irony all at once,
Anna stretched out her arms as if to show satisfaction
in having single-handedly
infused the zest of life into yet another day or, perhaps,
she was weary at having
done just that for so long.

And the woman, who taught me to dance life's tormented tango,
ascended and began
to disappear from sight, I saw her face, one last time...
that face, which had captivated me so many years ago...

She was looking back at me with her inscrutable smile,
her sparkling eyes illuminating the dark, elusive Roman night...
Until—she was gone.

*adapted from *Roman Nights*

CORAGGIO

I love to be on the top floor, up here...
like the whole city is mine!
Look—the Pantheon, the Colosseo, and over there San Pietro!
It's not just a view...it's home.
My home—the only place I ever feel like is really me, really my own.
My whole life I was passed around from my grandmother to my aunts to
        the nuns—
Ooofffaaaa!
A poor relative taken in for charity. Exiled.
I never felt like I had a real home.
But Roma, *Roma* is my home.
This city is like a beautiful woman;
the soul of a woman with the heart of a man!
Can you imagine me, as a little girl running around these streets?
No father, no mother...
People didn't know what to do with me!
They used to say: *'Guarda!* Look everybody,
it's the sister of Romulus and Remus!
A *bastarda* she is! *È una Lupa!* A She-Wolf!
I loved it! I thought I was so special—
I was able to forget all that happened and invent a new life...
I created myself, out of nothing, *out of nothing!*
That's courage, darling, *coraggio!*—that raging fire in the heart!
And when you have that, no one can take it away from you.
Because *coraggio* rises, like heat, like fire...it goes up—not down!
Up!
It rises through the blood and veins, courage ascends,
it takes you right to the top.

And that's what I want to give my son, the only thing I ever had—
'courage' and the one thing I always wanted—
'a *real* home'.

2 PHOTOS, 15 YEARS

(after two black & white photographs of Anna and Tenn)
for Chiara Ricci

Tennessee Williams and Anna Magnani

Anna Magnani embraces Tennessee Williams

I.   1952

Obsession's moving Muse
Sparks Destiny
Lost Sister (for him)
Loyal Man (for her)
Theatrical symbiosis;
Making Magic
With their light
For us in the dark

II.   1967

The uncomfortable end is near
Cruel Age (for her)
Critics Turn (on him)
Seeking psychic resuscitation;
Love is the life-raft
We throw out
For each other
And cling to

Part III

Fire Tears
Lacrime Fiammante
Deora Dóiteáin

"A journey is called that because you cannot know
what you will discover on the journey,
what you will do with what you find, or what you find will do to you...
And, furthermore, you give me a terrifying advantage...
You never had to look at me.
I had to look at you. I know more about you than you know about me."

—James Baldwin

"Let everything happen to you: beauty and terror.
Just keep going. No feeling is final."

—Rainer Maria Rilke

"Weight of Worth" Copyright Susan Bernarcik ©2020

CLIMBING INTO ME

I never knew for sure
If you would be waiting in my bed
You always managed to slip past the ever-vigilant landlady,
     Who ate too much and drank not enough.
You knew I never locked the door,
A perfect crime of passion; you made the bed only to
Climb into it and wait;
I'd arrive, after a night of tending
and attending bar(s),
My boozy breath, honeyed and panicked,
My nose nippy from the windy, winding walk home
along those cobblestone streets.

It was the 90s West Village of New York City
In the top floor studio that was
Out of *La Bohème,*
     Right on Jane Street;
     Just off the Hudson River

We both liked the idea of sleeping
With the river nearby;
The comfort of constant motion
In our queer world
         —erratic and verboten

You scared me often, in so many ways
My blood raced from the suddenness
Of you
Not so much in my bed, but in my life
And for a dwindling while we were lovingly lost
With no tomorrows, and only our endless tonights.

And somewhere in the jagged, vast terrain
of my 30-something untamed
heart, you found the space
to settle in.

ONCE A YEAR

The white Mayflies
Create a bright, silvery summer haze;

They dance and love.
A full life lived in just two days,

Those lighting nymphs lie
Months in a cool watery nest,

Every year new;
Relentlessly lusting with no rest

Much burned and learned
And lost through their brave catchless breath.

Nothing else sought
But the same sacred flight of death;

Time soon passes
These secret creatures of endless flight

Leaving comes soon;
As they cling to each other and the night

Their passing passion shows but once a year;
Enough to barely sustain them

Evanescent encounters
worth their weight in waiting,

and so the waiting is all they'll ever know...
And everything they fear.

MY JERUSALEM

*In Memory of the 1990s and the loving souls
we lost to AIDS*

...and when I crossed the street
I barely knew you
playing in my mind—the million ones you could be
I knew I loved this man
yet, my eyes had been deceived
getting closer it was cruel to see
the bitter truth of our common reality
your strength devoured by struggle
your beauty not diminished
but you are half the man
I'm puzzled when I see

You're a statue from a forgotten past
Shattered—with no reason
too young to be worn by years
how long does it take to smoothe stone
by tears?
So I offer what sunshine I have left
—radiating my fire within—
and give my crooked smile
still perplexed at 'why?'
I want to scream like a child,
into an empty coffee can
feel that dull echo of pain,
I remember a hurt not yet known
but somewhere deep inside of me,
a lingering premonition
and so—I hate my new memory of you

I cross the street
turn the corner
collapse against a brick wall on Jane Street
I tremble
and I wail

but the strength of stone
and the permanence of this wall
are no consolation
I mourn for all the empty homes in this village
the heart-shells, like spent ammunition
that litter these savage and weeping streets...
fighting the ceaseless war
that has devastated
my Jerusalem.

YOU ARE
SOMETHING
ELSE

*for Tennessee Wlliams
and that summer of '96*

We don't kiss;
You and I.
We collide, crash and burn, touch and turn
Into each other
and then hover...
      With you I
hang on the edge
of every word's curve
and comb the corners of your thoughts
Playing it close
to the vest
—A close call;
too close to call...
You.
      Oh, how I want to call you—
            But we are elephants in each other's bedrooms;

Your arm lays across my shoulders at the cafè
Like a trunk extending connection...
Passionate pachyderms with our matching memories
And supernatural attachments,
Passersby in our neighborhood zoo wonder;
We let them peer through the bars,
and leer at their fear
of something wild briefly contained...
They're trying to see
What they will never have or be,
      What the unfolding of our secret "we" explains.
          Audacious elephants in each other's bedrooms;

There is so much heat and bright in our dark;
it *comforts* us; the darkness;
our shiny, sheeny, slippery darkness,
wrapped in our ethereal blanket,
huddled close in our lost space,
safe from the trappings of the terrestrial.
              Comfortably caged elephants in each other's
              bedrooms:

My arm sways across your shoulders at parties
Like a willow branch stroking a chimney...
We so easily could catch fire...
It's exhausting attempting to prevent
the exothermic from occurring;
Attempting and preventing,
And preventing the attempting...
But our smoldering realization remains.
              Quietly burning elephants in each other's bedrooms:

We are wine when we are
Together alone...
Omega men
Playing on the desolate planet of bed
Falling vanquished on the floor,
Gasping, gazing up at the ceiling fan,
Wooshing, whizzing and whirling away the
Oppressiveness of our auspicious August air;
The closing closeness of those lingering locked-away days
And hidden midnights
Will leave me,   *(and you will leave me)*
forever hungry for summer.

       "Why Can't I Be You?"...
Listening to The Cure
Knowing there isn't one
for what we have; an impossible,

ineluctable desire that has no frame
or streetcar
or name
and lives under words
and on the rattle-trap tracks
between sighs, glinting in eyes
and often disguised, it festers in gestures
and jokes amongst shared tokes
leaving us both hungry; "as if increase of appetite had grown
by what it fed on."
      And we are restless, crippled elephants in each
      other's bedrooms;

The "we" when we're together
can never be
Reconciled with the "you" and "me"
we are...apart;
The cruelty of such magic; now you see "us;"
Now...you don't!
      We are desperate, disappearing elephants in each
      other's bedrooms;

But, now, the monosyllable of the atomic clock
is sounding more like a laugh,
as it conspires with the gravitational forces
that are fighting us.
You take the twisting turn of a wife and
with it, alter the shifting shape of my life;
  we are something else again.
Newton's Third Law is not to be scoffed at
as we fall—
victim to outside forces.
      Because "we" are something else...

After you leave...
And sometimes when your memory is lying next to me,

I run along that Streetcar's tracks, chasing the logistics of our love
and searching the syntax
of our sinful acts...

>   *But it's all leaving, leaving the temporary us...*
>   *that leaves us both starving, always*
>   *hungry for summer...*

Apart, we imbibe to survive—
Making inarticulate supplications,
Trying not to hope   (for us, a deadly luxury)
Waiting for the silent sound—that deafening *click*
Of the long awaited, unmade, long distance phone call
Asking too much of the unresponsive air...
I will not be a rudderless Skipper
          to your impenetrable Brick—

>   Now, we are vanishing elephants
>   vanquished to each other's guestrooms;

But, I am drinking of you, when I'm not thinking of you
already lost in the sea of memories of us two;
I'm grasping at straws that turn into thoughts,
Morphing into imaginary
Lovers' battles we have never fought...
Until I'm breathless as I realize:
Everything—every *thing*
               is something else.

WHAT REMAINS

(A Mosaic of Missing Pieces and People)

What Remains
Now?

You are gone...

Did you drop from the sky?
That day freedom lost control
the clouds fell in and
swallowed you whole
Searching you still...
You were not laid to rest
The ground filled with pieces
Of you.
Like a ravaged hope-chest
and the dust is not enough
to keep you undead
forever falling
Forever in my head.

Did you forget yourself?
And me, too?
Now, years ago
Again...trying to save the pieces
But they keep leaving you
And leaving me.
Day by day...saving the new puzzle
You keep creating,
Hearing the same routine,
Wondering when you'll stop
the game
And watching our ancestral tapestry
Unraveling.

Did something devour you?
In the 1980s

seeing you fade away, not like sunsets
Or rain storms
(too pretty a simile)
but you would come back
and then fade
away some more
Turning into a shadow
before my eyes
wanting to feed you, bring you back
make you fat
It wasn't enough...
Neither of us had immunity
Without your piece
so crumbled family unity.

Did you sneak away?
You always wanted to leave
Sixteen years waiting
It's selfish to want you to stay
still
With me...
Smacked by the thought
I was not enough...
I wanted to be, for you—
My skin still stings
From that fateful, fate-filled
Day into night
The first one is ever "the only"
And then you took your
Self away—
I'm left here...with a nameless
Heart hitch-hiking
The rest of this ravaged road.

We don't get maps
For the years and
lonely losses

So we wander; and wonder...
and wonder while we wander
As we carry our crosses
trying not to count
the gaining of our losses;

Am I meant to be a remnant?
>*The sparkling colored misshapen*
>*Seemingly meaningless pieces*
>*Are life...*
>*And the gray grout that runs throughout,*
>*Holding them tenderly together, the*
>*Rambling river of losses?*

I'm guessing myself into thinking:
Why have you all...
Gone?
Without ever knowing you took
with you, a piece
of me...

I am
What remains.

NO GOD TODAY

It wasn't so much the bloody vomit
that sprung forth like fire from her tired mouth,
which looked like an upside-down horseshoe
it wasn't even the studied cry on her face as she heaved forward with all her
        fight,
like a large pray animal besieged by lions
expelling the demons that burned and turned inside her.
Not even the growling, angry, thrusting noise that echoed from her belly
        through
her scratchy, ragged throat making me cringe with
impotence.

What I saw first—before it all—
Before her fall, was the fact that she was no more than 19,
with a distended stomach like that of the hungriest Somali...
Here on 23rd Street in Chelsea, in Manhattan, New York City.

She had no whites in her eyes. Just muddy crimson,
and honey yellow
swirled together in a terrible beauty called
neglected, unwanted, hated, pitied, spat upon, poisoned, misplaced,
forgotten, rotten, thrown out, kicked down, kept down, useless, misbegotten
Brown. Not black.
There is no black, no white either.
The milky wetness of bile held together,
bright bits of blood red
mixed with deep phlegm green—
Coughing up rough cuts—rubies and emeralds
And I prayed for black and white...perhaps even shades of gray,
but no.
This life is in color. Violent colors of the everyday,
burning themselves like red-tipped matches into my eyes.

She fell to her knees, like a Muslim being called to prayer by the Azaan.
"Allah Au'kbar!" "God Is Great!"
And he is, isn't he?

This is a perfect testament to such greatness.
Terrific, Epic, Horrific greatness.
Perhaps man's more so than God's.
Her nails dug into the pavement and scratched along the cement
creating a deafening sound of a bodily plea,
a hungry scream,
some religious experience.
A devotion rarely seen, never felt...
She was committed to her own destruction, but committed like I have never
        witnessed. I envied this strung-out saint,
jealous of the junky Joan of Arc
As she offered the last remnants of her viscera, pieces falling purposefully
        onto the ground,
on to the asphalt altar, before her, she raised her head.
With the triumph and amazement of a woman who had just given birth,
But such miracles would never be bestowed upon her.

She raised her head in thanks and praise...
for another heavenly experience
A transient transcendence allowing her to leave
the ache and agony
of her everyday life, even for just a few minutes.
Weariness hugging opulence...
shanty shoes, and harried hair,
crumbling clothes, and strife stained hands.
She is youth wrapped in old
A memory in the present, fading before my eyes.
Except for her face, I can't place her face,
I don't know if she had one
How do people get begotten and then forgotten?

She bowed her head and prayed for God's blessing,
a benediction of contradiction.
She lifted her head
a final gesture to some other presence, she sighed.
Making her way to her feet, satisfied,

content, almost renewed.
She had a sense of her devotion, obliged for the opportunity.
She stood up then slumped, wavering with cosmic emotion, as the spirit
        left her.
She was staggering still in awe
of herself and her devotion.

A consecration to pain, that seems Christ-like.
she is sacrificed...over and over again...
on the streets of New York.

Then I think what would God say...
And then I think again,
No God Today.

TEMPORARY BLINDNESS

A sonnet for Kevin Cleary, an excellent friend, IX-XI

What remains now? Through the dense air I cannot see.
You have gone swimming in space, away and out...
Or did you drop from the sky? As you flew about...
That day freedom went blind and lost control, losing me.
And the sky fell in, as we scattered together, attempting to flee.
While it swallowed you whole, ignoring your plea and shout
Scooping you up in flame and smoke, then tossing you about.
I stumble and search you still...As certainty crumbles into maybe

'Missing' they say, an empty word, as if you may wash upon the shore.
I wonder and wander, touching things familiar in my altered state.
Nothing is left, and the dust is not enough...so I welcome my fate.
As I discover too much lives above, beyond, unseen or in the core.

In the meantime, my heart holds you, keeping you safe and undead
But my cursed blindness has you forever falling, forever in my head.

LIKE ELEPHANT BONES AND TRAIN CARS

*an automatic poem for Josh Joplin and Kevin Cleary
and the year 2001*

When I see things together, connected, disconnected and wanting to connect...And wanting to be connected, hoping and missing, and hoping to connect but still missing, I think of trains...I think of train-cars, in the night, linked like elephants traveling to certain destinations,

And then I think how elephants stick together through their long, complicated, messy, muddy lives, they stick together like humidity on your face in July, it glistens, and looks like the shiny, shimmery silver metal of a train in the night, caressed in moonlight as it rockets and rolls from place to place to place...That's me and you...Like the various cars that link together in a train, we are sometimes separate, sometimes together, distinctive, individual, yet somehow very much the same...gold and silver in the same chain...Like train-cars, the same, often going in the same direction, and on occasion sent off into the frontier, stumbling through the unknown... rocking through the storm-ridden night. Yet always somehow knowing we shall link up, join arms or join tails, like those elephants I saw one time, not in a zoo but on safari...in the wild that is the jungle, sometimes lush and sometimes asphalt, but it's never your fault, when...we separate.

We will, we will! Join our arms, join our tails, join our trunks...and journey together once again, we will. That is a promise, not any ordinary one but an elephant one, and elephants don't forget, why should they? People do... that's true, but I won't...I won't forget because when I close my eyes...and moments when they are wide open...I see your tears, elephants cry, too... that's true—I've seen it happen...like when elephants go off to die, saying goodbye and going off to die, to rest with the other elephant bones because that's how they do it. They do it right because they don't die alone and they die with the bones of their loved ones...

I know you will, I know you would...caress and stroke and cry on my bones and I will, too, for you, I will clean your bones with my tears, just like they do—with the bones of their fathers and mothers, friends and lovers, we should all be so lucky, and so that is how I will remember you, keep you in my mind, my elephant mind, like a photograph taken of a locket found in a footprint sunken deep into the sands of a stretching coastline...The coastline where trains and elephants run along, sometimes side by side... My memory of you cannot fade, because it is like that photograph locked in a locket captured in a photograph, and kept your pocket, so it is forever— which is like the ring of this coffee stain on this paper as I write this for you...

Unlike joy, it's pain, a common pain that keeps us together, before, after, and during the storm. That storm, this storm, every storm; the one that passed and has yet to pass, and all of the passing storms...Nothing can wash us away. Not even after the stormy storms' raindrops which drop together, one following the other, like elephants, like the train cars rattle-trap trapping over the tracks, like rain-drops and tear-drops dropping... Nothing will wash us away...even after the trains stop running, clack-clacking and tracking, connecting and running and re-connecting...and the elephants have all turned to white-washed bones.

SLOWLY, BY SURPRISE

Swooshing down Route 138
in the backseat of a Blue Cab, safe for a moment
from the sins of last night
from dangers drunk away
from the big city eyes that watch me
from small town ears that hear me
from the extorted kisses I pretend to forget
from the lava simmering inside me.

The Bridges lead to sleep,
The Narragansett Bay flirts with me
But I nod until we are...
Cutting across America's Cup
I'm safer sailing through another traffic light
praying they all stay green.
Flash Forward:
the boats bob in the harbor
my fists are clenched though I'm not late for anything
the 'stop and go' is unnerving.

Cut Back To:
a dizzying kaleidoscope of
bodies and bars, bathroom stalls and cocktail napkins
Remembering, vaguely
enough to create this cold sweaty anxiety that dews on my temples,
I'm not wearing my sunglasses
—too cliché for a life so unplanned, the high of white knuckling everything—
it's more fun to run
on empty, and better to flee from the obvious and kill the redundant

The steely March morning sky
is mellow, kind to my exhausted, red-streaked eyes
I feel protected by the metal and glass that surrounds me
able to see, but not be seen
A quick right and we are sliding down Thames Street
I've done this before...

I couldn't bear to walk,
all those early morning eyes staring relentlessly
scrutinizing my iniquities with no privacy for my confessions
my little discreet indiscretions
no room for escape or to escape from;
alone, I still reek of my transgressions.

Turning towards Ocean Drive
To nature's persistent purification
Rolling down the window
I breathe, a heaving, deep breath; a sob of a sigh
as I fade to black and go on mental vacation

The cool, heavy air
blowing off the Atlantic...
and something as predictable
as a sunrise
catches me, slowly, by surprise.

IN A DARK AND DIZZYING PLACE

In a dark and dizzying place
She is seduced by
Carelessly climbing eyes
Intrigued by the graceless space
Of inelegant desire; brutal and barren
With no context for the want
But the naked need;

Catching the virile breezes
Of an inscrutable glance
Passing—it caresses
Her neck, her lips, her hunger
And she lingers longer on the chance
than she normally would.

For now, she is left waiting
With more hope than anticipation
For those winds to surge, again
And begin to take her in...

She turns back, again
Whoosh—hmmmmmm—whoosh!!!
Breasts, chests, faces, feet
The perfume of bourbon
Sobers her...enough to dance through
Every chance to gain an understanding
Of this dark parade, this murky march
...these eternal, nocturnal submissions,
And various infernal renditions that only seem new
Through the bottom of glass or the often
Forced laugh as the party goes on,
and on and on...
Dimly marching across abandoned hearts;
Close examination of the other body parts,
Blithely ignoring the souls' vacancies
And she sees it all—it's all she sees
From the front row seat

That never sits still...

>   *We are all so terribly beautiful when we're pathetic and alone;*
>   *Her loneliness is tragic to me; her beauty deserves company.*

As she moves, not-so-much forward
But toward, something like home
into the next unknown
Blustery gust
To taste her cheeks
Or just pass her by...

WILD BOY BLUES

That girl she tried to hold him,
the wild boy blue

I told her...
It's like trying to hold fire
and you know that's true

Nothing wild stays tame
too long
like we want it to

He came cattin' 'round again
New Orleans to Atlanta to Boston
He just breezes on through

She went runnin' after him,
What's a girl to do?

I told her...
We're just prisoners in our bodies
And y'all know that's true

Nothing wild stays tame
too long
like we want it to

Of course the days grow tired
so we try and make 'em new

It's the nights we choose
and we'll take them win or lose

I'll tell you like I told her
Stay away from wild boys and
You'll stay away from the blues

WANTING TO STOP, INSTEAD OF STOPPING

I kiss boys
                              —Who like girls;
It's my problem, my cross;
A longing for a lingering Judas kiss
Just long enough for me to miss
When it's gone

I kiss boys
                              —Who like girls;
What's your problem?
Forbidden kisses taste better
dessert before dinner
Getting the boy who likes girls
Makes you a winner
Of a game that has no end, or point
other than the thrill of the kill—
and the wild, taboo-terrain of thick
not-so-soft lips

I kiss boys
                              —Who like girls;
Is that a problem?

But Christ kissed boys, it's true—
He loved boundlessly
And I do, too
maybe it's my calling—
Or just something to talk about...
They always seem to find me
these boys who slowly,
secretly, seek me out

I kiss boys
Who like girls;
That's your problem!

And they get what they want

and deserve—
And me?
I get a piece of darkness few ever know,
a piece of fire, cool enough to hold
Until an unseen wind blusters briefly—but never long enough—
The flame is soon gone; the elements have conspired and turned
Against me, I know, because my hands are burned—
fingers that were just caressing,
tempting to go farther,
are now a whispering, blistering stigmata.

I kiss boys who like girls
And even though I know it's a problem;
Something smolders still
—trying to touch too much again—
Testing my will;
through another layer—beyond the roles
we've been taught to play
Longing to touch him again:
to feel through the tough, rough flesh
of the pain that remains on my cheek like a bloodstain...

I kiss boys

                        —Who like girls
It's a problem;
And I can tell you voluntary heartbreak
is not any easier to take—
I find myself fondling my self-inflicted wounds;
Bloodied pieces of my fist-sized muscle
mixed with the shrapnel of impossible passion.

Like the love child of Sisyphus and Prometheus
I am doomed to climb atop a new hill
to keep stealing that fire,
Creating secret "us" after secret "us,"
I'm unbound for now.
Soon to be rolling that flaming ball

Up a different mountain,
of which I never seem to tire

Eventually, I have to stop
kissing boys who like girls;
It's a promise I have to keep,
...Some day,

                          —kissing boys—

It's a habit I must drop
...Some way,

                        —who like girls—

Maybe, I'll finally stop.

LAYING US TO REST

for Vinny

"Never Forget..."
You said "I Love You"
Eye to eye
in that bright black of night
WHY?

When now you only hang in the dark
                    closet of my mind
Why should I relive that?
                    How can I forget
                    tormented by dangling visions
You told me to keep it.
                    Now you dance in darkness.
There are days I want to join you,
                    defy you, escape you
lose you...
                    How can I remember?
                    —without seeing bloody shadows?
Without feeling you are not here
and I was not there
                    Without trying not to breathe;
                    Without not wanting to?
You knew more than I did
                    Did you know what you meant?
I know better now...
                    You knew what you said!
I am numb again
                    'I love you' is dead
Maybe you saw something
                    I did not see.

But now I am no longer me.
What did you mean?
I hate that you loved me
I'm left behind and left over and left

Shivering; cold or fever?
The fear and delirium
Of living on a mental island

You have made me a Hamlet
Seeing ghosts and things evanescent,
Insane from feigned madness...
I reject affection from the new innocents
Making my bed of our aching sadness

I'm hoping you go away...again
Leave the corner you occupy
In my mind...
And try not to breathe
I try not to
Too deeply
I try not to breathe, I try not to leap, too
holding my chest, chasing what's left;

Only...if...
If only I had taken you down
              from your self-made cross
              of rope and steel
              to kiss you goodbye,
I could
              lay you to rest...

ANIMAL KIND

If you're not like me, who do I belong to?
I'm not like you, so where do I go?
A zoo, a prison,
an island of indecision.
Something must be done with me—for me—to me?
Can't throw me away, like some defective toy—
a mission gone bad—an aborted ploy...

Am I here to stay, until you decide?
Can you make me go away? I cannot hide...
Oh, what is to be done with me...
to me, for me, about me,
Help me!

You have known...Me...More than you'll ever Know...
You've known the grown Me...Less than light knows Shadow.
You want to disown Me...More than wanting me to go...

You see me like an animal that's betrayed you.

But we're family, and I'm not like you
I belong in a zoo or maybe a prison,
an island I cannot envision.
Keep your distance from my difference,
don't be fooled by silence,
it is not deference.

As darkest corners reveal themselves in gravest hours.
An open mind would leave you vulnerable to the disease
you try to stop from spreading—consuming you
like a tubercular love;
Your hate means nothing to death and
your mind is but one breath
in a world full of heavy sighs.

We have both left scathing moments, that scorch the mind
burning word-wounds that cannot be left behind...

But, I,
I am the one
Leaving my soul-blood in the shadows
Drops of eternity,
blots of my life left on the floor of my cage;
I want you to finally see me; Put your hands on my rage

So, now that your wishes have been shown, made known and carried out.
Where do I go now, where can I go? To be left alone, to live or die
like an animal...?

DRAGONFLY BOY

for you, and the summer of 1986

I'm ode-ing again, pining for summer, for another chance
At you; and the zig-zag freedom of dips in
Limitless water—soaring far through the balmy air.
Like the nymphs we are, care-free for now;
Along the edge we dance and amble
—it's a gamble, our lunar kisses in the dark,
A gambol of near misses in fits and starts—
Illuminated by the wet and heat we bathe in,
Where even just a little is so much more.

I see through you and
it makes you stiffen and shudder;
My eyes easily penetrate your translucent wings
Admiring more than your taut streamlined body,
I want to collect you, hold you briefly in my hands
Only to let you go again,
That's what we do, it seems—
Fly and flutter into each other
And then release...

Dragonflies don't know much what to do
With such strange, terrifying beauty that
So captivates the onlookers?
They desire to see us, to take in our shocking
Colors, and lightning-like movements.
They desire us near—to stare a fair while and touch a piece of
Ephemeral otherness,
Only to push us away when the prurient thrill is spent.
This hums true because I'm a Dragonfly boy, too

Hungry for summer, hoping
to soar with you
ride you bareback across the silver-black of night...
Our wordless spell—the lusty colors of magic—fading;
Summer somehow always runs out on us—

Our uncommon truth—the hungry, waiting whispers of want—
And only our wispy wings are swift enough
To keep the fall at bay;
To keep us hovering another minute,
leaving a little as we stay...
Until we dart away in opposing directions
Skimming over sand and sea
—while proposing some future connection—
Wanting to fly, to flee, to soar
Only one summer more.

THAT FIRST NIGHT

I'm night-walking
We are walking at night
in the village
It feels like the first time
but I've done this before
...I'm sure—or something like it—
The cold draws us closer
the heat makes us near
and fear keeps us warm
I want to see you
I may never know
I thought you want me
and so I'm thinking quietly

Don't tell me it's too late
          ...late at night
          ...night-walking
The neon signs
blinding, and I need fire for light...
The city swirls up and trips me
a plastic bag holds my leg
and begs me to stay,
so I smile and
it makes you a future in my eyes

The can you kick
plays my favorite song over and
over in my head
and leaves me wondering
if you even know—do you?

My feet feel good tonight
your hand looks right for mine
Could we pass 20 years?
Could we see always?

Night-walking

I'm walking at night
with you
Late...it's so late, this first
so-right night
As the city creeps out of darkness
To welcome us into the shadows of our soft secrets, and
I see you, stirred and swirling in
a sea of hurting,
and I saw myself too;
Do I seem beautiful...now?
I hope I do to you
Do you even see me?
This first night.

CAUGHT IN THE STORM
OR THE PAST UNREAL CONDITIONAL TENSE

If I was there...
If I were there...
If I had been there?

I would help you,
and hold you,
and calm you
I would pray you—
What elusive
storm brews in that
haunted mind
and devours your spirit
with such an
insatiable appetite?

If I was there
I would carry you
through such an
ominous gale,
and shield you
from any harm,
And together we would
look into the eyes
of that horrid tempest
that scares you
still...

If I was there
I would tell you
Sleep, Sleep,
my dear brother,
for such woeful weather
is over now,
the eyes of the storm
are shut,
the winds of fear and

the torrents of sadness
have all but subsided
and I am here
                    If I was there, no; no!
                    The verb tense is all wrong;
If I "was" then this poem would
not exist
and you would! I can't resist
pausing to obsess and wallow in the abstract,
to digress in the lost syntax of possibility.
If...the word keeps you alive in some
grammatical limbo,
a hypothetical hive
in which our unconsummated
love can still thrive.

If I was there...   but, I wasn't.

If I were there...   it's pointless now.

If I had been there...

If only.

SLOW (I HELD THAT NIGHT)

I held the night and prayed it would die slow
Sealing fate in what can't be held too near
Knowing all the while day would make us go

Our eyes spoke and kisses confessed all to know
Trading glimpses and moments without fear
I held the night and prayed it would die slow

Casually revealing things too painful to show
Your stormy eyes, blue torrents turned clear
Knowing all the while day would make us go

Aware of the rules, careful not to break the flow
Wanting to shred your shirt, trying hard to be cavalier
I held the night and prayed it would die slow

The kiss finally came and passion began to grow
Our synchronous desire was right, hot and shear
Knowing all the while day would make us go

And when you leave it shall be hard not to follow
Wanting to keep that gift of one stray tear
Waiting to hold close your sweet, airy sorrow
I held that night and prayed it would die slow
Knowing all the while day would make us go...

HADRIAN FOR 15 YEARS

It had been 15 years since their
Eyes,hands,lips had held each other
                    In that life-giving deadlock.
—17 years since they both fell
Hard   —one of those catastrophic head-on
                    collisions that makes
                    the cover of newspapers.

They were always the other's headline
                    They clung to each other like ink to bold
                    print,
Hung on the other's words as if
Everything in the world
                    —or at least first, big love—
was at stake.

And for a while it was.

They devoured one another in plain sight—
                    Because they always knew it would end;

Time is the enemy of
Impossible love.
And it would end.
                    Badly. Completely.
                    (if it didn't, would it end?)

Graduate degrees and
distant new cities
and the girl to whom he was engaged—
                    Awaited them like the voracious
                    crocodiles who gobbled up poor
                    Antinous.

                    And *I*?
I was Hadrian for 15 years.

15 years of forever...

Until this night wherein we
guessed the progress of the stars.

I like talking about us
In the third person;
You've become a "him" to me.

*(You are not so close to me that the syntax of our love is so off—No, wait...
our love's syntax is off because you're not so close to me)*

I no longer call you by the name I gave
you;
And that blank space where you sit inside me
Crushes me with its emptiness,
Like a rock in a tin can it rattles around,
With each thought of _____, a dent,
a noise

—the scars of our love's echoes—
A mutilating mark the stretches across
our nameless, shameless something that
I used to call "our two years".

But I've grown so used to the reverberating distance
That I'm not sure I can speak of us anymore—

But then, again, here you come...

When you walked in, we were 27 again!

We cried when we said "Hi" and
*Could we bear to smile when we'd say
"Goodbyes?*

Our souls awakened as if that first, deep wet kiss
was a baptism.

And our names were spoken
                              for the first time, again. Aristotle was
                              wrong;
Love is two tongues in one mouth.

And then you fell into me, or
Between my legs, as I sat at the bistro bar,
                              You stayed standing,
                              We interlocked,
Touching as if to reassure ourselves
                              that the other was real.

We had tricked time, for the moment
                              —you were mine, again?
                              Arms like tangled vines against
                              A crumbling wall
                              Holding onto everything!

We, the prisoners of passion,
had locked the clock out!
                              For three hours—
                              We conspired against it!
And while it plotted its revenge...
                              We reimagined its monosyllable
From *tick tick tick*
                              —*we* kissed and
                              cried each tick into oblivion—
To love love love!

And we held ourselves in the shadow
of that vacant victory
for awhile,
Eyes,hands,lips
locked;
Knowing we would soon be left with something
                              we could never talk about,

which is kind of like nothing...

And unafraid of your tears,
                      I resolved to be Hadrian for another
                      15 years,
Caressed by the din of a Piaf song
                              —Clinging.

Until, we were young again
And gone?

ALL-STAR DESIRE

for RDC, AMC, TMH, and KPK and your friendships

As a high school football player, I wanted to die
Every day;
Not kill myself...
Just die—
      A lot.
           End it all.
                    Be a hero.   (Not a queer-o.)

As a high school football player, I was an
All-Star;
I wanted to love among *all* those stars,
Not tread the earth among the constant fear;
I never knew the courage it took to wake up each day,
To not let the world know of the small explosions
That pulsed through my soul—the longings
For that unspoken unspeakable moment when
Everything is to be told
        and *he's* holding me.

At 17, the more I grew, the stronger I became
The less alive I felt
I was a faint fire in those wild, frozen ephebic woods
Waiting and wanting to warm anyone;
Comforted only by the warm whisper of coulds...
            I *would* do so much, I wanted
              To do so much more,
But my self-imposed exile was an outstretched, hungry hand
To no man's land.

Then I read *A Streetcar Named Desire*
And somehow saw myself some way in Blanche
I didn't want to kill myself.
The first boy I ever kissed did that—
the day after he leavingly set my lips afire.

(Yes; *Love...all at once and much too completely)* *
—I was an expanding galaxy of want—
My only need, desire.

I wanted more—than Blanche, and Brick, and Chance, and Lady...
So, I fell, impossibly, for a cool, college
Bad-boy (my Gatsby who was far too busy
                Plucking Daisies to notice me)
And chased him for two love-sick years
living on the sustenance of his insouciance,
My own sweet necrotizing hope,
and our secret soaked kisses
That unbearably whispered '*maybe*'.

When I was a high school football player
I wanted
More to hide than be seen;
And I wanted more to be dead than alive;
But then I learned;
Death...the opposite is desire, *
And I wanted so much more than to just survive,
To be so much more than just alive;
I wanted...SO MUCH....
I wanted
              To be someone's fire—
                          I wanted
More
          and more
and   more
To be
          desired.

*lines spoken by Blanche DuBois from *A Streetcar Named Desire*

THE TOUCH THAT MATTERED   1

It didn't matter he came into my world days after his father
dropped dead in the driveway.
It didn't matter that the fatherless 14-year-old turned into the sensitive
       16-year-old
before my watchful eyes.
It didn't matter that he found in me what he'd lost in life's motions,
and I was fumbling for the son that was lost in space.
Two uncertain people seeking a certain moment of grace.
It didn't matter that he had cried in my arms.
It didn't matter that he required a reassuring hand on his back.
It didn't matter his stutter disappeared around me.
It didn't matter he needed me, more desperately than I knew...
It didn't matter.

When *the* call came;

None of it mattered...

THAT TOUCH THAT MATTERED   11

That day I was summoned to the headmaster because
A young girl lodged a complaint against me;
"uncomfortable" with my closeness with
Or *to*? "a certain male student"
She was disturbed by the fact
I put my hand on his shoulder.

Every queer teacher's nightmare
unfolding in this
crucible of high school hormones and school-girl crushes;
      I am Blanche DuBois—
      I am Tom Robinson—
      I have the Scarlet Letter...
And I am swiftly tainted
Painted with such a broad sinful stroke.

Suddenly, I am thinking that *distrust is the only defense against betrayal*
      (My general mistrust of non queers
      tells me someone is always angling to hurt me,
      knock me down, and put me in my place
      or destroy me)
And it all comes true this day with that touch.
That touch
That somehow mattered.

The boy—*ah, yes, it had to be, didn't it?*
For this tawdry tale to spin out in its ineluctable
destructive conclusion—
Never complained; never even knew of the feckless girl's
Anonymous, venomous, reckless accusation.

My life—devoted
      To helping young people see some light in letters
      To finding their way, their voices
      To making their way, their choices—
About to unravel without a court or witness or gavel.

Suddenly, slyly a vicious teenage girl is trying
to destroy me;
        In my head, the painful refrain I hear
        —over the 2am telephone line—
                "Pervert! Faggot! Queer!"
        Stabbed into my ears
        (again and again)
        like it's 1985...

I won't be a victim (yet again) to the vile
Bile and lies that fall from razor blade lips.
The Love War continues; it never ended really—
only pieces and fragments of peaceful reprieve.
But, I believe Whitman, *All truths wait in all things,*
While evil, too, lurks in the most unlikely place,
A boss, a priest, a teenager
Clad in leather, wrapped in satin, sometimes in lace

But I channel my Irish Granma, who fought daily battles
For eighty-something years, facing so many faceless fears
from The Falls Road to Wall Street
Life is about deciding, where you want them, she'd say,
At yer throat or at yer feet.

And I know my answer, so watch yourself.
I know my loving touch was loving;
I know *how* it was felt and that it mattered.
I know well it tried to make whole,
A teenage life that had been shattered.

THAT ELLIPSIS

At 23, I don't want my life to be
That cryptic ellipsis
At the end of chapter two
Of *The Great Gatsby*...
I will not be that for you
      —an ellipsis in the nick of time,
        I won't let myself get carried away, too
I won't *be* Nick Carraway this time—

I don't want to be trapped in an elevator
Of Fitzgerald's luscious lascivity—
Never having what I want;
Only ever able to touch, to see
Not even knowing my hands
Are on *that* lever of mystery?
      —Falling floors to find myself in my drawers
      in a Room (not Of One's Own)
      With a man I barely know,
      Baring special parts of my soul—

I will not live between deafening dots that
Dare to define me...
That repress my aggressive transgressions...Or
Warn the world with a Parental Advisory
Against my language and nudity
I will not live the life of that reclusive elusive
Ellipsis that You gave me,
Out of fear of my fluidity
The world will just have to
Catch up to me

I will not live between those
Deafening dots
That dare to define me...
      (I will not sit up straight
      Attempt to be a colon:

Or, manipulate and reduce myself
Try To Be semi;
And no, I won't be a common comma,,,
Always looking for... more?
I will be an ellipsis on my own terms—
Mysterious and evolving...
I will be myself. Period. Three times!)

And, finally,
I will not be
one of *those* ellipses.

LEOPARD CUB LOVE

I've loved you like a leopard cub
      From the day you stalked into my classroom—circling the desks—
      staring at me...
You soon began wreaking your happy havoc in a stagnant place
      That unknowingly longed for you. And
            I dared to connect the spots on your camouflaged coat;
                You were just like a lone, lost leopard cub,
                   Separated, savage, and solitary.
                       We're leopards, you and me.

I picked you up and carried you in my gritted teeth, slapped you around
      With a tender paw,
            Until you fell into line.

That day I spotted you injured, growling in pain on the school's savanna,
      I leapt down from my classroom tree and roared onto the plain, to
      protect you,
            My cub, who, somehow, unreasonably, seemed, now, a part
            of me.

Why did I choose you—*and you, me*—to let in that late spring?
      When leaving for summer break
            You asked me to "bring it in" for that first hug—I held you,
            and, miraculously, knew
                That what life, loss, and lost love had long
                denied me,
                   Destiny had laughingly fulfilled...
                   (Like a dozing pentomino puzzle-
                   player, you were a missing piece I
                   pretended wasn't necessary.)

I still don't know why you accepted my queer, childless, lone-leopard heart
      That I so long thought unworthy of a son's love.
            But...Answered prayers have a way of prowling
                Into our empty rooms so quietly.

Your trust I've cherished holding;

The phases of your feral youth,
        I carry like secret treasures unfolding.
You, not of my flesh but of my soul;
     That singular, silent prayer that—in being answered—
        Made me whole.

WHEN WE LOSE ONE OF YOU

for the kids we've lost

When we lose one of you
it is like the death of all of you
Everywhere and the death of us, too.

When we lose one of you
It's a hurricane, walls crash down, buoyancy disappears and we drown
When we lose one of you
It's an earthquake, we're shook and broken, the ground beneath swallowed
When we lose one of you
It's an explosion, all of our delicate certainties swiftly shattered

The teenage mind, with its throbbing amygdalae
and burgeoning prefrontal cortex—its rather hip hippocampus,
does not quite know that you—all of you, each of you—
Are the center of so many universes.

Leaving us to self-incriminate that our love for you
was much too little and a little too late
As we mourn the loss of an inimitable mind,
—your holy spirit, your magical soul—extinguished
before it even caught fire
Not yet ready to transubstantiate.

THERE IS TIME HERE

after Jamaal May
for my troubled ones

There is time here,
So much time here
Not just the act of spending it.
Or giving and taking it.
But real, honest to goodness,
Gracious time
To listen, to sit, to hear, to—
Right here...
Time
Like you find between
everything that is
really something else;
Like the student who comes to you
with a four-page suicide note and a plan
of action...
And tells you: *I want to die,*
            I haven't slept for weeks,
            I feel like I have cement in my head,
            I am worthless,
            And I just want it all to end.
And, suddenly, slowly
Time is all you have
Time is all *I* have
to give
I am time...
It's no longer a metaphor
for missing things or wanted moments, or lost feelings
for what's missing or wanted or lost
It's everything,
Time
And his unfledged heart is beating in my hands
And time is me holding it tenderly...
And whispering something that
sounds like

Hold on,
It feels red like
I've got you
It tastes salty like
I won't let go of you
Because I know life happens
Slowly, and
Loss? Happens always
Suddenly.

And, no, it's not time that is money
This clock does not tick off dollars
but real tears and heard heartbeats
        He's telling you: *You're the only one I trust*
And *I* understand that my Time is really light;
Is really something missing, like
Light shattering silence
—that silent unutterable darkness
Broken by touch—
Broken suddenly, slowly by a touch,
Screaming wordlessly
with an army of tenderness.

But they keep saying,
How *hard* my job must be
They keep telling me *never* put your hands on a child
—or else...
                (Or else, what?)

I am trying to say,
I still give my Time
all of it, everything, everything and
as much of *it* as I can,
to be time.
And...anything else that *needs*
To *Be*
Something else.

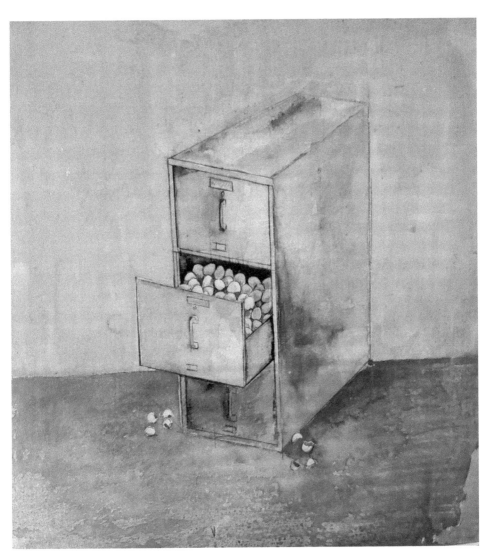

"Saved for Later" Copyright Susan Benarcik ©2020

"So moments pass as though
they wished to stay.
We have not long to love.
A night. A day."

—**Tennessee Williams**

ACKNOWLEDGEMENTS

My ongoing gratitude to my early writing mentors
Joseph Papaleo and Edward Albee;

Big thanks to Leah and Kevin Maines, Christen Kincaid;
the Finishing Line Press team; and Dankeschön Sabine Neufeld;

Grazie mille to the brilliant artist and my lifelong friend, Susan Benarcik;

An infinite *merci beaucoup* to Pamela Rader, my partner in literary and
culinary crimes, and my editrix extraordinaire.

Grá agus Buíochas to Mary Cronin, who first encouraged me to put pen to
paper.

Love and thanks to both my biological family with which I was blessed;
and
My logical family of which I am blessed to be a part.

ABOUT THE ARTWORK

I have known artist Susan Benarcik since 1985 and in 1987 we spent several months in Siena, Italy studying together and traveling the country. Since then we have always been connected through friendship and art. Years later in 2003, while I was teaching in Rome, she joined me for some more Italian adventures. It is an enduring and inspiring friendship of which I am very proud. Throughout these 35 years, I have found that Susie's dynamic and organic work speaks to me on a soul level that often seems to be directly taken from my own thoughts and emotions. It is through Susie that my friendship with Edward Albee, who also admired and collected her work, was fostered. In fact, in the summer of 1998, both Susie and I were awarded residencies at "The Barn" (Albee's famed artist residency) where we spent a month writing and painting and bonding.

Susan Benarcik is an artist deeply rooted in horticulture and her concern for the environment is made evident in her sculptural installations, prints, and surface designs. Susie has been creating art literally her entire life -we both share a compulsion to create. Most of the images in this book are from my private art collection, which includes five of her pieces. I hope that they speak to you and you see why they speak to me; I hope, too, that you see the subtle connections that have tied us together during the very period in which many of these poems were written. Whether in my Jane Street apartment (where I lived for many years) or my Newport townhouse, I have always been surrounded by books and art—they are a great comfort to me. So much of Susie's work incorporates the human form amidst nature as well as text; for me, the pages of a book have always been like leaves of a tree, so there is some type of synaesthetic symbiotic connection that we share. In keeping with his collection's thesis of "everything is something else," it is no wonder, then, that the natural world that infuses Susan Benarck's work is akin to the literary world that infuses mine.

—FMD

ABOUT THE ARTIST

Susan Benarcik is a sculptor and urban garden designer based in Delaware. Her work has been exhibited across the country in galleries, museums, sculpture parks, arboreta, and botanic gardens such as the New York Design Center, Brooklyn Botanic Garden, and the Delaware Art Museum. The artist is the recipient of Individual Artist Fellowship Award from Delaware Division of the Arts in 2019, a National Endowment for the Arts Challenge America Grant to Organizations and Artists in 2017, and a Pollock-Krasner Foundation Award, in 2007

The artist's concern for the environment is made evident as she takes elemental forms of the natural world into her studio and carefully transforms them by stacking, stringing, layering, knotting, and weaving them into contemplative works on paper and sculpture for public and private spaces. These interior and exterior compositions become part of our daily cognitive experience, and bring equilibrium to our senses.

The artist has a Master's degree in printmaking from Cranbrook Academy of Art, and a Bachelor's degree in Fine Art with highest distinction from Rosemont College. Benarcik was an apprentice at the Fabric Workshop and Museum in Philadelphia, a Core Fellow at the Museum of Fine Arts in Houston, and most recently a CFEVA fellow. She continues to design and install sculptural compositions while teaching creativity workshops in Delaware, Pennsylvania, and New York. The artist is a founding board member of the Jester Artspace in Wilmington, DE.

Her works can be found on line at inliquid.org, and on the artist's website: susanbenarcik.com

ABOUT THE POET

Irish-Italian-American playwright and poet **Franco D'Alessandro** is a native New Yorker and speaks fluent English, Italian, and basic Gaeilge. D'Alessandro has had twenty-two international, Off-Broadway and regional productions of his work and has been published or produced in eight languages over 11 countries on four continents. His Off-Broadway hit play *Roman Nights* explores the tumultuous lives of stage and screen legends Anna Magnani and Tennessee Williams. This play was a critical and commercial success in New York (2002) and London (2004); various productions of the play have been touring much of the world ever since, including a two-year run in South America and 15 year-run in the *Czech Republic and Eastern Europe*. *Roman Nights*, which has grossed over $1 million in box office receipt, has been running somewhere across the globe every year for the past 18 years and will soon be made into a feature film.

D'Alessandro's poetry has been published in various American and international literary journals and in September 2009 his poetry chapbook *Supplications: Immediate Poems of Loss and Love* was published by Finishing Line Press. In Fall 2011, *Stranger Love: Five Short Plays* was published; both books were immediately selected as Book of the Month by its publisher and have been endorsed by the National Italian-American Writers' Association and Irish-American Writers & Artists. They are available on FLP.com, Amazon.com and at the prestigious Drama Bookshop in New York City's theater district. In addition to his work as a playwright and poet, D'Alessandro is an LGBTQ equality activist and holds a Master's Degree in English Education and teaches high school English at the prestigious Bronxville School. He also teaches drama and theatrical text analysis as an adjunct professor at several universities and conducts Master Classes in American Drama at various conservatories—here and abroad—during the summers.

Franco D'Alessandro is a three-time Eugene O'Neill Playwrights Conference Semi-Finalist, a two-time Edward F. Albee Foundation Residency recipient, an NEA/TCG Playwrights Nominee, a two-time Dorset Theater Colony Residency recipient, a New Frontiers Playwright, a Cherry Lane Theatre Alternative Finalist, and a Princess Grace Award Nominee.

Mr. D'Alessandro is a proud member of The Dramatists Guild of America (1996), the Irish-American Writers & Artists, the Italian-American Writers Association, The Cherry Lane Playwrights Alternative, and the Writer's Guild of America.

Everything is Something Else marks the first major published collection of D'Alessandro's poetry.

He lives with his partner, Michael Milek, in Bronxville, New York.

Visit: www.francodalessandro.com
Facebook: Playwright-Franco-D'Alessandro
Follow on Instagram @IrishItalianFrankie

"You wouldn't want to be minding them poet fellows,
they're a dangerous clique be the best of times."

—Brendan Behan

My fingertips do
The speaking
That my lips
Dare not do

ALSO BY FRANCO D'ALESSANDRO

DRAMA

Find Me An Angel
The Beauty of Exile
Mothers' Day
Dying From The Details, Is That You or Is That Me?, Before & After
Roman Nights
Solo Anna
The Shattering
Maximum Happiness: 2 Two-Act Plays
The Museum Hours Trilogy:
(Finding Magdalene, Lifting Antaeus, Overlooking David)
White Elephants Dancing The Flamenco
The Darker Side of Paradise
Stranger Love: Five Short Plays
The Claddagh Ring Cycle:
(Dancing Barefoot, The Bronze Son, Trouble Me)

POETRY

Supplications: Immediate Poems of Loss and Love

ESSAYS

Tennessee and The Roman Muse: The Inspired Friendship of
Tennessee Williams and Anna Magnani
Diana Descending: A Portrait of the Fiery Oriana Fallaci
Infinitely Isabella: An Intimate Interview with Isabella Rossellini

"Animal Kind" Performed as a monologue in the play "Is That You Or Is That Me?" by Franco D'Alessandro, 2001.

"Life's Tormented Tango: The Last Moments of Tennessee & Anna" and "Coraggio: La Casa di Anna" are extracts from the stage-play, **Roman Nights**, by Franco D'Alessandro ©1998, 2001.

"Like Elephant Bones and Train Cars" first published in **Balancing the Tides**: *A Newport Arts Journal;* III Edition, 2007.

"Out Of Place" and "Crawling Up Into Eternity / Il Colosseo" first published in **Balancing the Tides**: *A Newport Arts Journal;* IV Edition, 2008-2009.

"Anonymous, But Not To Me", "The Sandbox," "Like Elephants and Train Cars," "We Didn't Yet Understand," "The Wake Too Soon," "What Remains," "Laying Us To Rest," "Temporary Blindness," "You Are Something Else," "Roma," "Crawling up into Eternity," & "Slow", all previously published in the Chapbook **Supplications:** *Immediate Poems of Loss and Love* by **Franco D'Alessandro**; Finishing Line Press, Lexington KY, 2009.

"The Returning Immigrant" previously published in *No Distance Between Us—The Next Collection*, 2020.

ADDITIONAL PRAISE

"This book is an important collection of poems by a gifted playwright-poet, in the tradition of my dear friend, Tennessee Williams. Give your beleaguered soul a break; read Franco D'Alessandro's *Everything Is Something Else!*"

   –**Bruce Smith**, Author, *Costly Performances: Tennessee Williams— The Last Stage*

"It is as though D'Alessandro has invested millions in life and squeezes every penny returned. The poet sits in the middle of his poem (as he does in his plays) speaking loudly about persons who matter. You will read *Everything is Something Else* many times over... It is healthy to be exposed to such passion!"

   –**Gregory Abels**, Director, Poet, & Zen Master

"Touchingly beautiful, hauntingly fragile, creating memories of lost loves and present passions; Franco D'Alessandro's profoundly poignant poetry goes deep down into the depths of the soul and whispers, 'I am here, I see you, let's make some beauty from our pain'."

   –**Bina Sharif**, Playwright, Artist, & Director

Franco D'Alessandro, through his artfully crafted words and deeply felt emotions, realizes perfect illuminations that portray his conception of life full of his *veri af etti*-true affections. The author's words try to "maybe to find, but more to see" what his life has left inside him and, even more, what life still has in store for him. And it will be an amazing discovery without end for him and for us. This is D'Alessandro in all of his profound and moving honesty.

   –**Chiara Ricci**, Ph.D., Author of Vissi d'Arte, Pres. Piazza Navona Cultural Association

"Born of 'Roman blood and forged in Celtic fire,' D'Alessandro's poetry inhabits that precious middle distance between the spiritual and corporeal. While being present and reflective at once, he reminds us that we are all fastened to this earth, to each other, and to our collective condition.

   –**Josh Joplin**, Songwriter, Singer, & Lyricist